Gordon Ramsay
A chef for all seasons

with Roz Denny

photographs by Georgia Glynn Smith

introduction by Charlie Trotter

TEN SPEED PRESS
Berkeley | Toronto

For my three little stars - Megan, Jack, and Holly.

May you all grow up to love food as much as I do.

Page 2: Salade Tiède of Mushrooms,
Mussels and Crosnes (recipe on page 128)

Ten Speed Press
P.O. Box 7123
Berkeley, California 94707
www.tenspeed.com

Library of Congress Cataloging-in-Publication Data is on file with the publisher.
ISBN-10: 1-58008-742-6
ISBN-13: 978-1-58008-742-1

Printed and bound in Singapore

2 3 4 5 6 7 8 9 10 — 09 08

contents

Every once in a while a chef comes along whose personality and clarity of vision help to revitalize people's interest in cuisine. Gordon Ramsay is just such a chef. He is truly one of the top chefs in the world. His innovative combinations of ingredients produce remarkable results. A former professional athlete, Gordon has transferred his physical intensity and passion from the gaming field to the gorgeous plates he creates. As with any great chef, he does not merely concentrate on the visual aspects of food, he focuses on flavor and the visual follows naturally. Gordon's dishes are alive with purity and elegance. They remind me of why I love to cook. He has the ability to connect himself to the purest essence of foodstuffs. The resulting flavors are poetic, even haunting.

With this book, home cooks and professionals alike will delight in discovering new and intriguing ways to combine the wealth of each season's harvest. Gordon's recipes are imbued with the vital, sensual nature of the cooking and eating ritual. Each of the four chapters in this book excites a season's best. The introductions contain odes to the freshest and best of each time of year, as Gordon lovingly describes his favorite foodstuffs. The *Spring Pea Soup*, for example, is a dish that not only encapsulates his integrity of flavor, but its exquisite simplicity allows the fresh peas to shine, with the smoky hints of bacon providing the perfect accompaniment. Equally intriguing is the *Baked White Peaches with Thyme Ice Cream*. Luscious peaches, picked at their perfect ripeness, call for little alteration, save that of creamy, lightly-scented ice cream. It's difficult not to constantly lick your lips as you thumb these pages.

Another reason I am partial to Gordon and his food is our shared Scottish heritage. Some consider Scots to be a bit rough and headstrong at times, but it is always in the pursuit of excellence. I have reason to believe that deep down Chef Gordon is a big softy. In fact, I've watched him cook and I must report that Gordon Ramsay is as gentle as a lamb when preparing one of his scintillating dishes.

Charlie Trotter

spring

Spring starts in my kitchen around March. The cold winds may still blow outside, but our spirits are lifted when the suppliers start to bring in treats from the warmer South of France. The lengthening of the days and the anticipation of the best of new season's produce perk us all up in the restaurant kitchen.

One of the first foods to appear are sweet **peas** in pods. They are so tender that you can just pop the pods and scoop out the tiny peas to eat raw. In France, housewives like to cook the peas in their pods because the pods are tender and full of flavor. I have a particular fondness for peas, as they were the first vegetable I was allowed to prepare in a Paris kitchen, when I was promoted from sorbets onto "veg" prep station. I had truly arrived! Peas are great with fish – I use the bigger ones puréed in a fish velouté. I am not wild about peas served cold, although I remember once enjoying a pea vinaigrette with cold lobster in Paris.

In the days of nouvelle cuisine many chefs were accused of using baby **carrots** (and other baby veg) only as a garnish. The criticism haunted many of them, but now young carrots are back in favor, no longer on the back burner of fashion. Available for about six months of the year, baby carrots first appear in spring, and we are able to get excellent locally grown carrots, straight and full of flavor. We just scrape them and cook lightly in butter with a splash of water. They're terrific with spring lamb, of course, but also try them with a braised fillet of cod, or cut them into thin julienne strips and serve them as a vegetable "spaghetti." Another idea is to cook them briefly and then souse in vinaigrette to serve cool.

To my mind, the Rolls Royce of spring vegetables are baby *fèves*, or **fava beans**. In France, they are used as a luxurious garnish, or cooked in the same way as new peas – in the pods for a soup. My days at Jamin, Joël Robuchon's restaurant in Paris, saw me spending hours preparing *fèves* for the light, fantastic "cappuccino" of *fèves* with baby lobster, one of the favorite spring appetizers on his menu. I've also eaten them as a warm salad with grilled cuttlefish. *Fèves* have a lovely earthy taste, and are good in many country-style dishes, such as with potato gnocchi or a salad with ricotta. Peas and *fèves* together make a good plateful, complementing each other in every way. While one is sweet and tender, the other is fuller and more "meaty" in texture. They work nicely as a twosome.

In top kitchens, **baby leaf spinach** now enjoys a designer-label status, but many trainee chefs make the mistake of boiling and squeezing the life out of the young, delicate leaves. If my young *commis* want to please me, they just check for bruised leaves and stray weeds. When it comes to baby leaf spinach there are lots of don'ts: don't pinch off the stems, don't wash roughly, don't crush in a spinner, don't boil smothered in water, and, please, don't

ever squeeze or chop the wilted leaves. The best of the best baby leaf spinach comes to us in the spring. We dress it simply in vinaigrette or cook it just with a tablespoon of water and a bit of butter. Sometimes it is so delicate that we simply put a small mound of fresh leaves straight onto a piping hot plate. They wilt instantly and that's all the cooking needed.

A vegetable that is featuring more in my cooking is **bok choy**, which is a pretty Chinese cabbage with stems that look like Swiss chard and a flavor that is a glorious blend of spinach and artichokes. Our supplies come in at the end of spring and continue well into midsummer. We cook the baby-size ones whole, allowing one per portion. They make a great presentation vegetable with roasted poussins, grilled John Dory, or poached salmon. Bok choy is also ideal for stir-frying, as it cooks in seconds in a hot wok.

If *fèves* are the Rolls Royce of spring ingredients, then I'd describe **white asparagus** as a Ferrari on a test drive, because it disappears so fast. Even white truffles have a longer season. I get really excited when it comes into the kitchens. The pearly-white cigar shapes have a gentle, delicate flavor, much kinder on the palate than the more robust green asparagus. The stalks need just a little peeling. We always serve white asparagus as whole spears, often simply dressed in vinaigrette. The French adore it with chicken (*poulet de Bresse*, of course) and some sautéed morels.

In season for much longer than white, **green asparagus** is particularly good as a garnish for main dishes. The stalks are often woodier than white spears, because they have a lower water

content, so we peel almost the whole length, to nearer the tips. Our usual preparation is to blanch and refresh them, and then reheat in a little buttery water just before serving.

Root and tuber vegetables have a special place in our culinary repertoire. Up among the most favored are **Jerusalem artichokes**, which, although available year round, we enjoy using in early spring. Despite the name, they are not botanically related to globe artichokes, and they have nothing to do with the Holy city. It seems that the name is somehow derived from the Italian for sunflower (*girasole*), which is what they were called when they were introduced to Europe from North America. Both Jerusalem and globe artichokes were popularized in Europe by the French, who still use them in many different ways. Jerusalem artichokes need very little peeling (which is a good thing as they are knobby, like a juicy root of fresh ginger) and have a rich, velvety texture when cooked. We take advantage of this and use them to make sublimely smooth soups. Blanched and then sautéed in a little butter, the roots color up beautifully.

Spring marks the arrival of, for me at any rate, the ultimate mushroom – the **morel**. I must have expensive tastes because my favorite ingredients (white truffles, white asparagus, and morels) all have a very short season and resist fruitful cultivation, no matter how hard clever gardeners try. For us, fresh morels are around for just four to six weeks. They have the strangest shape and look like spongy, brown woolly hats. Morels are quite tricky to clean, and need light scrubbing (like white truffles) and quick rinsing. We stuff the larger ones with a chicken mousse and use the smaller ones in sauces. Needless to say, I do enjoy eating them with spears of white asparagus, simply dressed with melted butter or a vinaigrette.

During March and April, my supplier, Mark Bourget, comes back from Italy with new season's **garlic**, which he gets from the mountains in the north. These have smaller heads than normal garlic and taste sweeter. But they still have an overpowering pungency, which can kill other flavors in a dish. You can tame this by blanching the cloves several times in boiling water. The leaves of new season's garlic, which look a little like mint leaves, can be shredded to mix into risottos at the last minute, or added to dishes of beef, lamb, or robust fish such as halibut. I like to *confit* garlic cloves, unpeeled, in goose fat, then fry them until the skins become nice and crisp.

We use a lot of **parsley**, both curly and flat-leaf. Curly-leaf has a very pronounced flavor, which is mellowed by blanching in boiling water. This intensifies the glorious dark green color, too. Once the blanched parsley is refreshed in ice water, we squeeze it dry and then purée. This parsley purée is mixed into creamy potato, whisked into sauces for fish and oysters, and even used as a light thickener. Flat-leaf parsley is ideal for garnishing, as it has a pleasant cleansing effect on the palate. It should not be chopped too fine as it bruises easily. Recently we have started serving it with sardines tossed in vinaigrette, and we also deep-fry sprigs for a fish garnish.

Chefs are sometimes accused of popularizing cod so much that stocks are threatened by demand. Well, while I love cooking cod, I also enjoy other white fish. One is **whiting** (it's my Mum's favorite, popular in Scotland). Flaky and full of flavor, it has the strength of cod with a slightly softer flesh, making it brilliant for a *brandade*. Although the flesh is quite soft, it is not at all watery if really fresh. The American silver hake is sometimes called whiting, but this is a different (and finer) fish.

For me, baby-size **poussins** – also called spring chickens even though they are available year round – are just right for light spring menus. We find people prefer to eat them at lunchtime, but not dinner, possibly because they seem lighter. My favored cooking method is what the French call *poché-grillé* – we poach the birds whole in broth to par-cook them, then remove the breasts and legs and pan-roast them. That way the meat remains succulent and the flavor is enhanced by browning in a hot pan.

When it comes to meat cookery, spring is the season for new **lamb**. Somehow, heavier meats such as beef, game, and, to a certain extent, pork seem not quite appropriate for this time of year, while lamb appeals. It is tender, sweet, and delicate in flavor, and the outside cooks in next to no time to a wonderful caramelized, almost barbecue flavor.

Our supplies come from a number of areas, depending on the season. I prefer Scottish and Welsh lamb in spring and, when possible, use milk-fed lamb. During the fall, I like to get in lamb from the Pyrenees, in France, where it is reared almost completely wild; later on in the season it takes on a more gamy flavor, like wild boar. Lamb is the most versatile of all meats. We use the little legs, "cannons" from the saddle (especially popular with our lady customers), and rib chops, and also the shanks for braising.

I have to confess, I'm a **Granny Smith** man because it is such a well-balanced apple – sweet and sharp with a firm, juicy texture – and it is as good raw as cooked. We use it for many desserts – in iced parfaits, in fruit salads, and as a sweet *jus* for our hallmark dessert, crème brûlée, by crushing the apple flesh at the last moment to make a simple sauce. And that's not all. Sliced wafer thin, dipped in stock syrup, and then dried overnight, Granny Smiths make excellent (fat-free) *tuile* cookies. You can't get a more versatile ingredient!

In late spring, small fragrant **apricots** with blushed pink skins begin to feature on our supplier's list. The apricots come from France and Spain, two countries that offer a number of wonderful recipes for this amazingly versatile fruit. We use it in both savory dishes and in desserts. In my early days at the Aubergine, we had a pork dish with stuffed apricots on the menu, which won many fans. Clafoutis with baby apricots is a light, easy dessert, or the fruits can be poached in a little cinnamon- and anise-scented syrup to serve with creamy rice pudding. The supply of small apricots lasts until the start of summer, when larger fruits arrive. These we make into a chutney to serve with foie gras (like the Peach Chutney on page 213). Out of season, we use half-dried French apricots (what the French call *mi-cuit*) that need no pre-soaking. They are brilliant for jams.

The exotic fragrance of **mangoes** is simply wonderful. When buying, don't choose a mango that is too ripe – you need an edge of sharpness to balance the luscious sweetness. For savory cooking,

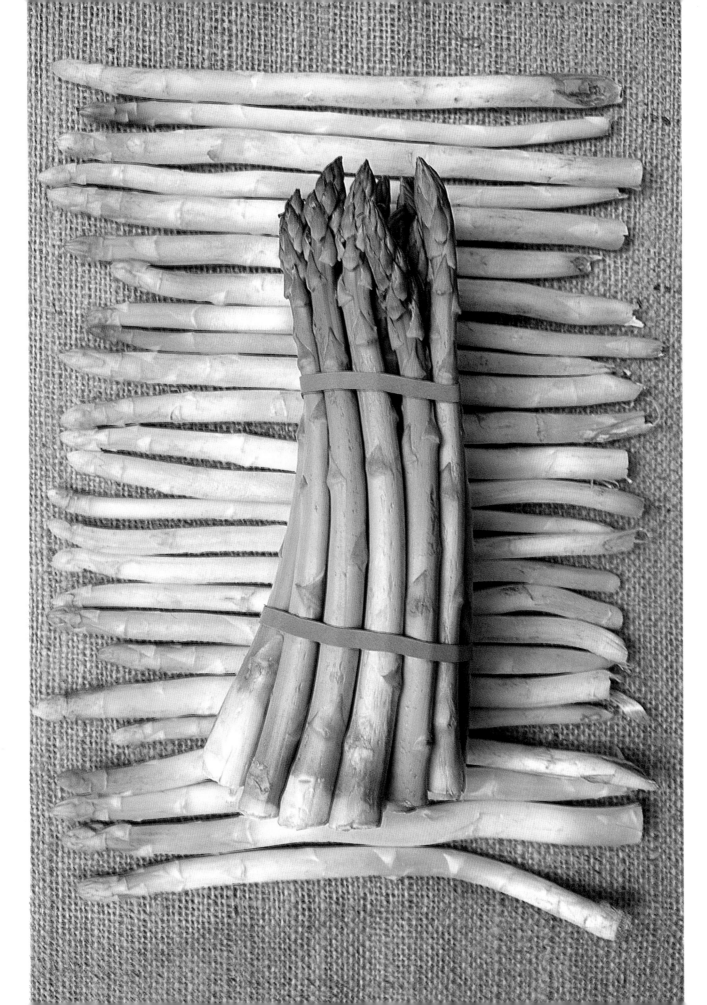

buy fruits that are hard and slightly acidic. Match them with sweet seafood or with chargrilled chicken or pork and a hint of aromatic curry spices. Underripe mangoes also make good relishes and chutneys. In the dessert menu, mangoes go well with butterscotch flavors, but my ultimate favorite "marriage" has to be with coffee and cream, which we use in a sweet ravioli recipe. For this, peel a large, firm mango and cut wafer-thin slices. Soak them in stock syrup for a couple of hours so they soften, then drain and pat dry. Make a filling from seriously strong espresso coffee, thick crème fraîche, and softly whipped cream, sweetening slightly. Scoop this into balls and lay between the sheets of softened mango.

I could wax lyrical about **rhubarb**. In spring we get tender, day-glo pink stalks, which are sometimes called "forced" rhubarb because they are grown in hothouses or covered with tall pots (this makes them grow straight and tall). We can generally get rhubarb all year round. Until the late 1940s, this plant was classified as a vegetable, but it is now called a fruit. I use it as both. As a vegetable, we fry rhubarb and mix with *choucroute*, or use it to make a fantastic sauce for fish and lobster (this is quite a talking point at any dinner party) – sauté the chopped rhubarb in a little butter with salt and sugar, simmer gently in Vegetable Nage (page 212) to a purée, then mix with some vinaigrette. Another savory idea is to sauté rhubarb in butter, then deglaze with grenadine syrup and serve as a quick relish for foie gras or pan-fried liver. For me, the nicest sweet way to cook rhubarb is roasted with sugar, butter, and vanilla, to serve with crème brûlée or a lovely rice pudding.

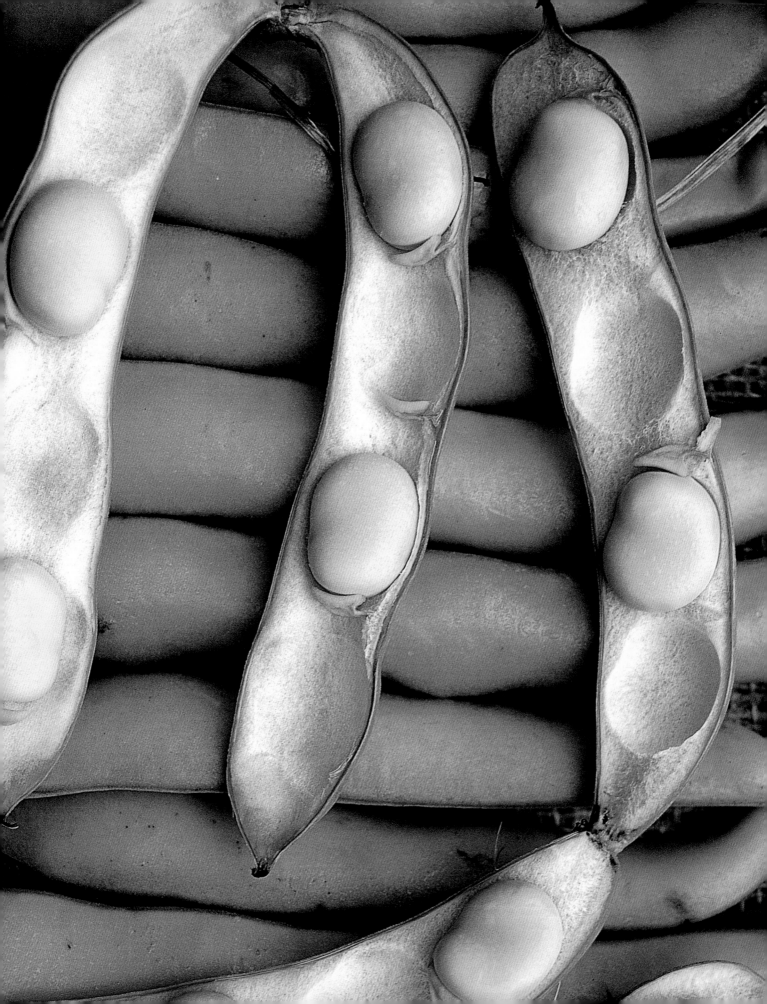

Spring Pea Soup

This is a light, creamy soup that has everything going for it – a tempting color, velvety-smooth texture, and a wonderful fresh flavor. Pea and bacon are a popular combination. I like to use Ventrech bacon from Alsace, but another lightly smoked, dry-cure bacon would be fine.

SERVES 4 AS A FIRST COURSE

4 ounces lightly smoked sliced bacon

2 shallots, sliced

2 tablespoons olive oil

1 pound fresh peas in pods, shelled

2 tablespoons dry white wine

4 cups Light Chicken Stock (page 212)
  or Vegetable *Nage* (page 212)

½ cup heavy cream, plus a little extra for serving

Sea salt and freshly ground black pepper

1 Reserve 4 slices of bacon and chop the rest. Place the chopped bacon in a saucepan with the shallots and oil. Heat until sizzling, then sweat over a low heat for about 5 minutes.

2 Add the peas and cook for a further 2–3 minutes. Pour in the wine and cook until it has evaporated.

3 Stir in the stock or *nage* and 1 cup of water, and bring to a boil. Season, and simmer for 15 minutes. Blend in a food processor or blender until smooth, then pass through a fine sieve into a bowl, rubbing with the back of a ladle. Leave to cool and then refrigerate.

4 Meanwhile, broil the reserved bacon slices until crisp. (In the restaurant we bake the slices between two heavy baking sheets to keep them straight and flat, but you may prefer the crinkly look.) Drain well on a paper towel so they aren't greasy. Keep warm.

5 When the soup is well chilled, check the seasoning and whisk in the cream. Season again. Serve in bowls with a little extra cream trickled on top and a floating bacon slice.

Jerusalem Artichoke Soup with Morels

Once regarded as a boring winter vegetable, Jerusalem artichokes are now enjoying a revival and are back in fashion. At New York's Daniel restaurant, they just scrub the roots rather than peeling them. You can do that for this soup, which will give it a rustic, pale gray-beige color. If peeled, the soup will be paler.

Fresh morels have a very short season, so you should try to make the most of them when they're available. We always prepare them at least an hour before cooking, washing them very carefully – ours are grown in sand, and even a few grains can ruin this sublimely smooth soup – and then leaving them to dry. Out of season, you can use 2 ounces dried morels, first rehydrating them in warm water. **SERVES 4 AS A FIRST COURSE**

5 ounces small fresh morel mushrooms

1 pound fresh Jerusalem artichokes

Juice of 1 small lemon

3 tablespoons olive oil

2 shallots, chopped

½ cup dry white wine

4 cups Light Chicken Stock (page 212)
  or Vegetable *Nage* (page 212)

²/₃ cup heavy cream

2 tablespoons butter

A little freshly grated nutmeg

Sea salt and freshly ground black pepper

1 Cut the morels in half lengthwise, then rinse well in cold running water to extract all the sand. Pat dry on paper towels and leave for 1 hour to dry completely.

2 Either scrub the artichokes or peel thinly with a swivel peeler. Fill a bowl with cold water and add the lemon juice. Cut each artichoke into slices and drop immediately into the acidulated water (this will stop them browning). Leave to soak for 5 minutes, then drain and pat dry.

3 Heat 2 tablespoons of the oil in a large saucepan and gently sauté the shallots for 5 minutes. Add the artichoke slices and cook for another 5 minutes.

4 Add the wine and cook until it has all evaporated. Pour in the stock or *nage*. Bring to a boil, season, and simmer for 15 minutes or until the artichoke slices are softened.

5 Blend in a food processor or blender, then pass through a sieve, rubbing with the back of a ladle. Return to the pan and mix in the cream. (At this point, you could chill and freeze the soup to serve later.) Heat until on the point of boiling, then set aside.

6 Heat the remaining oil with the butter in a frying pan and sauté the morels for about 5 minutes, stirring often. Season and sprinkle with a little freshly grated nutmeg. Drain on a paper towel.

7 Reheat the soup, if necessary. Ladle into four warmed soup plates and scatter the morels over. Serve quickly. No garnish needed, save the morels – simple and sublime!

Asparagus Soup
with Fresh Cheese Croûtes

The lightest of spring soups, this has dainty floats of chèvre and mascarpone croûtes made from a ficelle *(thin baguette). The soup can be made ahead and then reheated to serve.*

SERVES 4 AS A FIRST COURSE

1 pound fresh green asparagus
2 tablespoons olive oil
1 medium onion, minced
1 small carrot, minced
1½ tablespoons butter
2 sprigs fresh thyme
4 cups Light Chicken Stock (page 212)
  or Vegetable *Nage* (page 212)
Sea salt and freshly ground black pepper

To serve
1 *ficelle* (thin baguette)
2 cloves garlic, peeled
Light olive oil for shallow frying
4 ounces semi-soft chèvre, rind
  removed
1 tablespoon mascarpone

1 Trim the base of the asparagus spears, and use a swivel peeler to peel the skin from the stalks if a little tough. Cut off 12 tips about 2 inches long. Chop the rest of the asparagus.

2 Heat the oil in a large saucepan and gently sauté the onion and carrot for about 5 minutes. Add the butter and, when melted, stir in the chopped asparagus and thyme. Sauté for 5 minutes, then cover and sweat over a low heat for a further 15 minutes until the asparagus is nicely softened, stirring occasionally.

3 Pour in the stock and add some seasoning. Bring to a boil, then cover and simmer for just 5 minutes – this keeps the flavor fresh. Check the texture of the asparagus stalks – they should be very tender. Remove the thyme sprig.

4 Lift the vegetables into a food processor or blender using a slotted spoon, reserving the liquid in the pan. Blend until creamy, slowly adding the liquid to the processor bowl. For a velvety texture, pass the purée through a sieve back into the saucepan, rubbing with the back of a ladle. Check the seasoning and set aside.

5 Blanch the reserved asparagus tips in boiling water for 2 minutes, then drain and plunge into a bowl of ice water. Drain again and set aside.

6 To make the pretty croûtes, cut the *ficelle* into ½-inch slices. Allow 2–3 slices per person. (You may not need all the bread.) Rub the slices on both sides with the garlic. Heat a thin layer of oil in a frying pan and, when hot, cook until golden brown and crisp on both sides. Drain immediately on paper towels and cool.

7 Beat the chèvre with the mascarpone and season lightly. Spread in attractive swirls on the croûtes.

8 Reheat the soup, check the seasoning, and pour into warmed soup bowls. Float the croûtes and asparagus tips on top and serve.

Spinach Velouté Soup with Goat Cheese Quenelles

Velvety-smooth, vibrant green, and very simple – just the pure flavor of the vegetables topped with a light and silky cloud of goat cheese and mascarpone with chives.

SERVES 4 AS A FIRST COURSE

1 pound fresh leaf spinach
2 tablespoons olive oil
1 medium potato, about 7 ounces,
   peeled and thinly sliced
A little freshly grated nutmeg
4 ounces fresh soft goat cheese
   (about ½ cup)
3 tablespoons mascarpone
1 tablespoon chopped fresh chives
⅔ cup heavy cream
Sea salt and freshly ground black pepper

1 Pick over the spinach, discarding any large, tough stems and bruised leaves. Wash the remainder well in two changes of cold water, then shake off the excess water.
2 Heat the oil in a large saucepan and sauté the potato for about 5 minutes until soft. Add the spinach and stir it over the heat until well wilted.
3 Add 4 cups of water plus seasoning to taste and a little grated nutmeg. Bring to a boil, stirring. Partly cover the pan and simmer for about 15 minutes, stirring once or twice.
4 Meanwhile, beat the goat cheese and mascarpone together until softly stiff, and fold in the chives. Season if you want to. I don't. Set aside.
5 Ladle the soup into a food processor or blender and blend until smooth. Pass through a sieve back into the saucepan, rubbing with the back of a ladle.
6 Stir in the cream and slowly bring to a boil. Adjust the seasoning. Simmer for a minute or two.
7 Ladle the soup into warmed bowls. Shape the goat cheese mixture into quenelles, or just carefully drop spoonfuls in the center of the soup, and serve immediately.

Variation

For a special occasion, I sometimes make this soup with oysters. I shuck eight, saving all the juices. The four largest oysters I poach gently in the juices for a minute or two, then drain, reserving the juices. The other four I blend in the food processor with the spinach and potato mixture. All saved oyster juices are added at this point. When the soup is served, I place a poached oyster in the center of each bowl and spoon the goat cheese mix on top.

Pillows of Ricotta Gnocchi with Peas and Fèves

If you have the impression that gnocchi is doughy and boring, then let me persuade you to try making potato gnocchi. They are much lighter than semolina gnocchi. Anyone who enjoys pottering about in the kitchen and cooking should have a grand time with these!

SERVES 4 AS A FIRST COURSE

2 pounds large boiling potatoes

1¼ cups all-purpose flour, plus extra
  for shaping

1 tablespoon fine sea salt

1 teaspoon freshly ground pepper
  (preferably white)

1 egg, beaten

½ cup ricotta cheese

5 tablespoons butter

1⅓ cups shelled fresh peas

1⅓ cups shelled fresh baby *fèves*
  (fava beans)

3 tablespoons Classic Vinaigrette (page 213)

2 tablespoons chopped fresh parsley

Sea salt and freshly ground black pepper

1 Boil the potatoes still in their skins until just tender. Drain and peel them while hot. (We do this wearing rubber gloves to protect our hands.) Cut each potato into quarters and spread out on a baking sheet.

2 Dry off in the oven preheated to 400° for about 5 minutes. Then mash until smooth. The best way to do this is to push the potato through a ricer. Failing that, a masher will do, but not an electric mixer or food processor, or the texture will become gluey.

3 Mix the potato with the flour, fine sea salt, white pepper, egg, and ricotta cheese. The mixture will be like a soft dough. Don't overbeat or the gnocchi will be tough. Spread out the mixture on a plate and chill until firm.

4 Shape the potato mixture into long cigar shapes about ½ inch thick. Using the back of a table knife, cut across into 1¼-inch lengths. (See photographs of this technique on page 220.) Bring a large pan of water to a boil. Add the gnocchi pillows and simmer for about 5 minutes. (You may have to cook them in batches.) Drain well and plunge immediately into ice water. Drain again and pat dry on paper towels.

5 Melt the butter and heat slowly until it turns a light brown color. Strain through a fine sieve and discard the solids. Pour the butter into a frying pan and lightly fry the gnocchi until nicely colored all over. Season and keep warm.

6 Meanwhile, cook the peas and *fèves* in lightly salted boiling water for 2–3 minutes. Drain and season. Stir in the vinaigrette to bind and then the parsley.

7 Divide the pea and *fève* salad among four plates and top with the browned gnocchi. Serve immediately.

Warm Salad of Cèpes and White Asparagus

White asparagus is popular in Europe, where it is associated with fine dining. The spears are almost always served whole. Between April and May, I am able to buy plump white asparagus grown in the Vale of Evesham, in England. It is so tender there is no need for any peeling, just a thin trimming of the stalk end. It makes a good simple salad, topped with sautéed sliced cèpes and a brown butter sauce. **SERVES 4 AS A FIRST COURSE**

About 12 large spears, or 24–30 thinner
  spears, fresh white asparagus
Juice of 1 lemon
¼ cup olive oil
5 tablespoons unsalted butter
7 ounces fresh cèpes, bases trimmed, sliced
2 tablespoons fresh flat-leaf parsley leaves
Sea salt and freshly ground black pepper

1 Prepare the asparagus first. Trim the ends. Bring a shallow pan of salted water to a boil and add half of the lemon juice and a tablespoon of the oil. Add the asparagus spears and blanch for about 4 minutes, then drain carefully (so as not to damage the tips) and plunge into a wide, shallow bowl of ice water. Leave until cold, then drain carefully again and pat lightly dry.

2 Make the brown butter: Heat the butter gently in a small saucepan, then turn up the heat and cook until the butter just turns brown. Watch it like a hawk! Tip it quickly into a cup to stop the browning. Set aside.

3 Heat the remaining oil in a frying pan and fry the cèpes, stirring and tossing, until just softened. Add the parsley leaves, season, and remove to a plate.

4 Wipe out the pan and tip in the brown butter, leaving the solids behind in the cup. Heat very gently, then lay in the asparagus spears. Heat carefully until hot, then sprinkle the rest of the lemon juice over.

5 Arrange 4 asparagus spears on each plate, drizzle any pan juices over, and spoon on the cèpes. That's it – naturally simple.

Salad of Avocado and Crab with Pink Grapefruit Dressing

You cannot beat classic combinations of flavor and color – avocado and seafood win fans every time. But instead of a creamy mayonnaise-style dressing, try mixing the seafood – here crab – with a light vinaigrette spiked with star-burst bubbles of pink grapefruit. The pastel shades and fresh flavors will make this a very popular appetizer.

Fresh crab meat is the best choice. If you have to use frozen, press the crab meat in a colander using the back of a ladle, to remove all excess liquid. **SERVES 4 AS A FIRST COURSE**

1 pink grapefruit

²/₃ cup Classic Vinaigrette (page 213)

2 large, just ripe avocados

2 plum tomatoes, skinned, seeded, and chopped

Juice of ¹/₂ lime

1 teaspoon minced shallot

Few drops of hot pepper sauce (optional)

5 ounces white crab meat (about 1 cup)

About 4 ounces small salad leaves
  (a mixture, or mâche or small wild arugula leaves alone)

Sea salt and freshly ground black pepper

1 Cut the peel and pith from the grapefruit, then, using a sharp fruit knife, cut between the membranes to release the sections. (Do this over a bowl to catch the juice.) Add the sections to the bowl and break into tiny "teardrops" with the prongs of a fork. Mix in ¹/₂ cup of the vinaigrette and set aside.

2 Make a guacamole: Halve the avocados, remove the pit, and scoop out the flesh into a shallow bowl. Mash to a chunky purée using a fork, then mix in the tomatoes, lime juice, shallot, pepper sauce to taste (if using), and seasoning.

3 Carefully check the crab meat for any bits of shell. (We do this on a flat plate with the back of a fork.) Season nicely and bind with 1 tablespoon of the remaining vinaigrette.

4 Toss the salad leaves with the last of the vinaigrette, and season too.

5 To assemble the salad, use a large, plain biscuit cutter 3 inches in diameter. Place the cutter in the center of a medium plate and spoon in one-fourth of the guacamole. Lightly press one-fourth of the crab meat on top, then make little towering piles of salad leaves on top of that. Gently lift off the cutter. (See photographs of this technique on page 221.) Wipe the cutter inside, and repeat three more times on three more plates. (Alternatively, you can simply spoon the three salads on top of each other on the plates.)

6 Finally, dribble tiny teaspoonfuls of the grapefruit dressing around each salad and serve.

Steamed Scallops and Asparagus with Lemongrass Butter Sauce

Whoever said steamed food was boring? Not me. For example, I love the pure, delicate flavors of sweet scallops and pencil-thin asparagus steamed in their own juices, then gently coated in a fragrant beurre blanc. Try to buy the scallops in shell (have the fish merchant open them for you), so you have the cup-shaped shells for cooking and serving. In the restaurant we usually throw away the corals, but you can cook them if you wish. SERVES **4** AS A FIRST COURSE

4–6 sea scallops, shucked,
  with 4 of the rounded shells saved
5 ounces thin green asparagus tips
1 tablespoon chopped fresh chervil or chives
Sea salt and freshly ground black pepper

Sauce
1 stem fresh lemongrass, tough
  outer leaves stripped off
2 shallots, minced
½ cup dry white wine
1 teaspoon white wine vinegar
2 tablespoons heavy cream
½ cup (1 stick) unsalted butter, chilled
  and cut in small cubes

1 Rinse the scallops well and pat dry. Feel for the hard nugget of flesh on the side and pull this off. Very plump scallops are best sliced horizontally in three, otherwise simply slice in half.

2 Scrub out the shells and divide the asparagus among them. Season lightly and place the scallop slices on top, adding the corals if you are using them.

3 Prepare a pan of boiling water over which your bamboo steamer will rest. While the water is heating, make the butter sauce.

4 Mince the lemongrass, discarding any hard, woody bits. Wrap and tie up in a piece of cheesecloth. Cook the shallots and lemongrass in the white wine for about 5 minutes until nicely softened and the liquid has reduced right down to almost nothing. Remove the lemongrass bag. Add the vinegar and cook until evaporated, which takes seconds.

5 Stir in the cream, season, and bring to a simmer. (The cream helps to stabilize the sauce.) Drop in a couple of cubes of butter and beat vigorously with a small whisk until melted and emulsified. Drop in some more butter cubes and whisk again. When all the cubes have been added, mix in 2 tablespoons of cold water and remove from the heat. Cover the top of the sauce with plastic wrap or a butter wrapper and set aside to keep warm.

6 Bring the pan of water to a good head of steam. Season the scallops and place the shells in the basket base. Place over the pan and cover with the lid. Steam for 3½–4 minutes, depending on how thick the scallops are.

7 Remove the basket from the pan – take care as steam can burn badly. Lift out the shells carefully so as not to spill any juice, and put on plates, setting each shell on a small mound of rock salt. (The salt helps to keep the shells level so they don't tip over.)

8 Coat the scallops with the butter sauce, sprinkle with the herbs, and serve right away.

Whiting with a Lemon and Parsley Crust

The crust for this fish is made in an ingenious way. Instead of pressing a loose mass onto each fillet, it is pressed together as a sheet, cut, and placed on top. Then the fish is cooked half submerged in liquid, with the crust poking out at the top. To complete the fresh green theme, you could serve the fish on a mound of baby leaf spinach. Just place the spinach on piping hot plates so the leaves wilt – no need to cook. **SERVES 4 AS A MAIN DISH**

1 large whiting or silver hake, about
   2¹/₂ pounds, filleted in four, skin on
3 tomatoes, skinned, seeded,
   and minced
3 tablespoons olive oil
3 tablespoons coarsegrain mustard
1 bay leaf
2 sprigs fresh thyme
3 tablespoons heavy cream
Sea salt and freshly ground black pepper

Crust
1 cup (2 sticks) unsalted butter
4 cups unsweetened brioche crumbs
   or good-quality white bread crumbs
2 cups curly-leaf parsley sprigs
Grated zest of 2 lemons

1 Check the fillets for any pinbones, then cut each across in two to make eight pieces. Set aside.

2 Cook the minced tomato in 1 tablespoon of the olive oil until you have a slightly chunky purée. Season and set aside.

3 Make the crust: Blend the butter and crumbs in a food processor until crumbly. Drop in the parsley, lemon zest, and seasoning, and blend to fine crumbs. Line a wooden board with plastic wrap and tip the buttery crumb mixture on top. Cover with more plastic wrap, and roll out with a rolling pin to a rectangle about ¹/₂ inch thick. Place this crust in the freezer to firm up for a couple of hours. Then cut into eight pieces about the same size as the fish fillets.

4 When ready to cook, preheat the oven to 400°. Spread 2 tablespoons of the mustard over the skin of the fish, then spoon on the tomato "purée." Finally, lift the crust cut-outs off the plastic wrap and press gently on top. Lay gently in a flameproof baking dish, crust-side up.

5 Put the remaining oil in a small saucepan with 1¹/₄ cups of water, the herbs, and seasoning. Bring to a boil. Pour the liquid down the side of the baking dish so it doesn't wet the crust. Bake, uncovered, for 8–10 minutes until the crust is light and crisp and the fish feels firm when pressed lightly in the center. Remove from the heat and, using a long spatula, lift out the fish onto four warmed dinner plates.

6 Place the baking dish on the stovetop and boil down the liquid by half, then add the remaining mustard and the cream. Pour neatly around the fish. Serve with baby new potatoes.

Roast Turbot with Asparagus Velouté

Turbot is one of the largest of the flatfish, with flesh that is both tender and quite meaty. Chefs love it because it is so accommodating and teams well with a variety of flavors. This is a lovely dish with which to welcome spring to your table, chic and yet quite casual in presentation.

SERVES 4 AS A MAIN DISH

1¼-pound fillet of turbot, skinned

8 ounces fresh green asparagus

3 tablespoons olive oil

1 shallot, chopped

Leaves from 1 sprig fresh tarragon, chopped

1¼ cups Fish Stock (page 212)

About 2 ounces fresh baby leaf spinach

2 tablespoons heavy cream

8 ounces tagliatelle (preferably fresh)

2 tablespoons butter

1 tablespoon chopped fresh chives

Sea salt and freshly ground black pepper

1 Cut the fish across into four even slices and trim to neaten. Set aside.

2 Trim the bases of the asparagus spears and peel the stalks, if necessary. Chop half of the spears into small pieces; reserve the other half.

3 Heat 1 tablespoon of the oil and sauté the chopped asparagus gently with the shallot and tarragon for 5 minutes. Add half the stock and a little seasoning, and simmer, uncovered, for 3–5 minutes until tender. Add the spinach and cook until wilted.

4 Blend the asparagus and spinach mixture in a blender or food processor until smooth. Pass through a sieve into a saucepan, rubbing with the back of a ladle. Mix in the cream and set aside until ready to serve.

5 Cook the tagliatelle in boiling salted water until just *al dente*. Drain, rinse under cold water, and drain again. Return to the pan with half of the butter. Set aside. (This is what we do in the restaurant, but you may prefer to cook the pasta later, while you are cooking the fish.)

6 Cook the remaining asparagus in lightly salted boiling water for about 3 minutes until just tender. Drain, rinse under cold water, drain again, and return to the pan with the remaining butter.

7 Heat the remaining oil in a large non-stick frying pan and, when hot, cook the fish for about 1 minute on each side until nicely colored. Season the fish as it cooks. Pour in the remaining stock and bubble gently, spooning the pan juices over the fish. This part-braising keeps the fish moist. After about 3 minutes, the stock should have reduced to a syrupy glaze and the fish will be just tender.

8 Heat the pasta, adding a splash of water if necessary to stop it from sticking. Season and toss in the chives. Reheat the asparagus spears.

9 Place the pasta in the center of four warmed plates. Meanwhile, reheat the asparagus and spinach velouté. Center the fish on top of the pasta, spoon the hot velouté around, and surround with the blanched asparagus spears. Serve quickly.

Sea Trout with Crushed Fresh Peas

Wild sea trout, like salmon, can live in fresh or salt water. Slightly sweeter than salmon and a little smaller, they are at their best between April and September. Superb fish needs just the simplest of accompaniments – in this case a crushed purée of fresh summer peas bound with a little vinaigrette and enhanced with some fresh marjoram. Serve with baby new potatoes.

SERVES 4 AS A MAIN DISH

1 sea trout or steelhead trout, 4^{1}/$_{2}$ – 5^{1}/$_{2}$ pounds,
  filleted in two, skin on
1–2 tablespoons olive oil
1 pound fresh peas in pods, shelled
1 tablespoon chopped fresh marjoram,
  plus marjoram leaves for garnish
2 tablespoons Classic Vinaigrette (page 213)
Sea salt and freshly ground black pepper

1 Feel the fish flesh for any pinbones with your fingertips and remove them with your fingernails or tweezers. Cut each fillet across in half. Trim these four pieces neatly. Using the tip of a very sharp knife, score the skin in thin parallel lines, leaving a ^{1}/$_{2}$-inch border uncut all around. Rub both sides of the fish with the oil and set aside.

2 Cook the peas in boiling salted water for 3–4 minutes until just tender. Drain and return to the pan. Crush the peas against the side of the pan with a fork so you have a chunky purée. Season, and stir in the chopped marjoram and vinaigrette. Set aside.

3 Heat a non-stick frying pan. When you can feel a good heat rising, place the fillets in the pan, skin-side down. Season, and cook for about 4 minutes so the skin becomes crispy. Carefully turn, and cook the other side for a minute just to brown lightly. Season again.

4 Spoon the crushed peas into the center of four warmed dinner plates and place the fish on top. Garnish with marjoram leaves, if liked, and serve.

Poussins with Baby Bok Choy in Sweet-Sour Sauce

Oriental flavors have been enthusiastically embraced in classic Western kitchens – it's all about culinary lateral thinking. I like to serve roasted poussins (a.k.a. squab chickens) with a sweet-sour sauce and tiny heads of Chinese greens called bok choy. Don't trim the bok choy – they are cooked whole. **SERVES 4 AS A MAIN DISH**

¼ cup olive oil

4 poussins, 1–1¼ pounds each

5 tablespoons butter, melted

8 small heads bok choy

2 tablespoons dark soy sauce

Sea salt and freshly ground black pepper

Sauce

1 red sweet pepper, chopped

1 yellow sweet pepper, chopped

1 tablespoon olive oil

1 tablespoon white wine vinegar

1 teaspoon sugar

3 tablespoons Classic Vinaigrette (page 213)

1 First, make the sauce. Sauté the chopped peppers in the oil for about 5 minutes until softened. Deglaze with the vinegar and add the sugar, stirring until dissolved. Blend to a fine purée in a blender or food processor with the vinaigrette. Rub through a sieve with the back of a ladle. Season and set aside.

2 Preheat the oven to 400°.

3 Heat 2 tablespoons of the oil in a large frying pan. When hot, add the birds, two at a time, and brown all over. (In the restaurant we press the poussins down with our hands so they color evenly, but this is only for the brave – or foolhardy!)

4 Place the birds in a roasting pan, open out their legs, and trickle the melted butter over, pouring it through a small sieve. Season. Roast for 15–20 minutes, basting the birds at least twice – spoon up the pan juices and trickle them through the sieve again. This gives the poussins an evenly golden, crisp skin. Spoon the juices inside the birds as well, if possible, for flavor. When cooked, remove from the oven and set aside to rest.

5 You can serve the birds whole, or you can serve them like this: Using a very sharp knife, remove the breasts from the bone in one piece. Cut through the thigh joint and remove the legs. We then loosen and pull out the thigh bone, leaving the drumstick, but you may find this just too much trouble! Discard the carcasses. Keep the meat warm.

6 Trim the bok choy neatly and sauté whole in the remaining oil for about 3 minutes. Deglaze with the soy sauce and season with pepper only.

7 To serve, place the bok choy in the center of four warmed plates and sit the chicken on top. Reheat the sauce gently and spoon over the chicken. This is nice with butter-dressed noodles, such as fettuccine.

Sirloin of New Season's Lamb with Lentils

This is a good homey dish similar to many served up and down France. We serve the lamb with creamy gratin potato. By par-cooking potatoes in milk before finishing them in ramekins, they cook more evenly. It's a neat little trick. **SERVES 4 AS A MAIN DISH**

4 thick lamb sirloin steaks or chops,
   about 7 ounces each
3–4 tablespoons olive oil
1 sprig fresh thyme
³/₄ cup *lentilles de Puy*
1 medium carrot
¹/₂ small head celeriac
1 medium leek
2 tablespoons coarsely chopped fresh parsley
¹/₄ cup Classic Vinaigrette (page 213)
Sea salt and freshly ground black pepper

Gratin potatoes
1 pound medium, slightly waxy
   boiling potatoes
1¹/₄ cups milk
1¹/₄ cups heavy cream
1 clove garlic, sliced
1 sprig fresh thyme
1 bay leaf
³/₄ cup grated Gruyère cheese

1 Remove the central bone from the chops. Trim off fat and neaten to nice "rump" shapes. Place in a bowl or plastic bag with half of the oil and the tips from the thyme sprig. Set aside to marinate in the fridge.

2 Cook the lentils in boiling salted water for about 15 minutes. Drain and season.

3 Cut the carrot, celeriac, and leek into ¹/₂-inch squares (we call this a *brunoise*). Heat the remaining oil in a saucepan and sauté the vegetables until lightly browned, 5–7 minutes. Mix with the lentils and half the parsley, then bind with 2 tablespoons of the vinaigrette. Set aside.

4 For the gratin potatoes, preheat the oven to 400°. Peel the potatoes and slice thinly (use a mandoline or the slicing blade of a food processor). Bring the milk and cream to a boil with some sea salt, the garlic, and herbs, and simmer for a couple of minutes. Add the sliced potatoes and simmer for about 5 minutes until just tender. Drain in a colander set over a bowl to catch the creamy milk.

5 Mix the potatoes gently with two-thirds of the cheese. Layer neatly into four medium ramekins or cocotte dishes, seasoning in between the layers. Spoon a little of the saved creamy milk on top of each ramekin and sprinkle with the last of the cheese. Place the ramekins on a baking sheet and bake for 8–10 minutes until the cheese just turns a golden brown.

6 Meanwhile, heat a heavy-based non-stick frying pan until really hot. Remove the lamb steaks from the bowl or plastic bag, wiping off any thyme tips, and brown for 3–5 minutes on each side, seasoning lightly as they cook. The lamb should be served lightly pink – medium rare.

7 Reheat the lentils and spoon into the center of four plates. Place the lamb steaks on top (slice them first, if you like). Deglaze the frying pan with the last of the vinaigrette, stirring for a minute, then spoon these juices over the lamb. Sprinkle with the remaining parsley. Serve the gratin potatoes, still in their individual dishes, on the same plate. Simple and delicious!

Oven-Roasted Caramel Bananas en Papillote

This is a seriously naughty dessert, so turn the page unless you wish to be tempted. If, however, you are still reading and cannot resist, then start to look for some sheets of parchment paper. Allow 2 medium bananas per portion. **SERVES 4**

¼ cup firmly packed light brown sugar
4 tablespoons unsalted butter
½ cup heavy cream
2 whole cloves
8 medium bananas, just ripe and not soft
A little sifted confectioners' sugar for dusting
4 stems fresh lemongrass
Crème fraîche for serving

1 First, make the caramel sauce. Melt the sugar in a saucepan with just a splash of water to get it under way. When dissolved and clear, raise the heat and cook for 3–5 minutes until a light-colored caramel is formed. Remove from the heat and immediately stir in the butter. Then mix in the cream and cloves. Set aside to infuse and cool.

2 When ready to cook, preheat the oven to 400°. Get four sheets of parchment paper ready, each about 8 by 12 inches.

3 Heat a non-stick pan until nice and hot. Cut the bananas in half lengthwise and dust with confectioners' sugar. Add to the dry hot pan and allow the sugar to caramelize on the first side before turning carefully. This should take just seconds if the pan is hot enough. (You may have to caramelize the bananas in batches, wiping out the pan each time.) As soon as the bananas are caramelized, remove immediately to the center of the sheets of parchment, allowing 4 halves for each serving.

4 Slash each lemongrass stem almost to the thick end and place on top of the bananas. Remove the cloves from the caramel and spoon it over the bananas.

5 Holding the two long ends of each sheet of paper up together, fold over and down several times, leaving a bit of a gap above the banana. Scrunch the ends in twists. Place the parcels on a baking sheet. (In the restaurant, we cut and fold the paper into "D" shapes and dust them with sifted confectioners' sugar before baking. The paper takes on a fantastic dark caramel gloss.)

6 Bake for 7–10 minutes until the parcels are puffed up. Serve each one on a plate, and just slash open the top to spoon in some crème fraîche. Serve as soon as possible. (Be careful when opening the bags to eat – they will expel hot steam.)

Easy Mango Tarts with Fromage Blanc Sorbet

The introduction of blowtorches into kitchenware stores has certainly made cooking more adventurous for the home cook! She (or he) can now make wonderfully quick caramelized toppings. This is one recipe where a blowtorch would come in handy. The base is puff pastry, which can be bought ready rolled. For the very best flavor, though, I suggest you make your own.

SERVES 4

1 pound puff pastry, preferably homemade (page 214)

Confectioners' sugar for sprinkling

4 ripe medium mangoes

2 ripe passion fruits

1 tablespoon chopped fresh mint

Fromage Blanc Sorbet (page 215) for serving

1 Roll out the puff pastry to about ⅛-inch thickness. Cut out four 5-inch rounds. (You could use a saucer as a template.) Place on a flat baking sheet. Prick the pastry rounds several times and chill for 20 minutes.

2 Meanwhile, preheat the oven to 400°.

3 When ready to bake, place a sheet of parchment paper on the pastry rounds and fit a heavy, flat baking sheet on top so the pastry is sandwiched in between. Bake for 10–12 minutes until dark golden brown and crisp. The baking sheet on top will keep the pastry bases flat.

4 Remove the top baking sheet. Dredge the pastry rounds fairly liberally with sifted confectioners' sugar and return to the oven to melt and glaze. Remove and slide the rounds off onto a wire rack to cool and crisp.

5 Peel each mango thinly and cut off two thick slices vertically on either side of the flat pit. Cut across the slices into half-moon shapes. Arrange on top of the pastry rounds, piling the slices toward the center.

6 Cut open the passion fruits and scoop out the flesh into a small sieve over a bowl. Rub the juice and pulp through. Trickle this over the mango slices.

7 Sift confectioners' sugar on the fruits, then immediately caramelize with a blowtorch. If you don't have a torch, then preheat the broiler until glowing red and caramelize the sugar that way. Take care, though, as the broiler could also burn the pastry edge.

8 Cool the tarts a little, then sprinkle with the chopped mint. Eat warm with scoops of fromage blanc sorbet or a bought sorbet.

Baby Apricot Clafoutis

This French favorite is normally associated with cherries, but I like to make smaller versions using fresh apricots. These start coming into season in late spring. We serve some almond ice cream alongside the clafoutis, but it is just as delicious served simply dusted with confectioners' sugar and topped with a trickle of cream or some crème fraîche. The batter mix is best left to rest and soften for a good 24 hours beforehand. **SERVES 4**

¹/₂ cup toasted sliced almonds
1 tablespoon all-purpose flour
Pinch of salt
¹/₂ cup granulated sugar
2 extra large eggs
3 extra large egg yolks
1 cup heavy cream
A little softened butter for greasing
12 ripe medium apricots
Confectioners' sugar for dusting

1 First, grind the almonds to a very fine dust in a coffee grinder or nut mill (it is hard to grind such a small amount of nuts in a food processor). Tip into a food processor and blend with the flour and salt, then add the sugar, eggs, yolks, and cream. Blend until smooth and creamy. Tip into a large measure and refrigerate for 24 hours.

2 When ready to cook, preheat the oven to 400°. Grease six round, straight-sided tartlet molds, 4 inches in diameter, with soft butter.

3 Halve the apricots and remove the pits. Cut each half in half, then divide among the prepared molds. Sift some confectioners' sugar over. Pour in the batter, and bake for 12 minutes or until risen and lightly firm.

4 Cool for a few minutes in the molds, then unmold onto a wire rack using a small metal spatula. Serve warm, dusted with a little more sifted confectioners' sugar and scoops of ice cream or spoonfuls of crème fraîche.

White Chocolate and Lemon Mousse

Yellow and white are the colors I associate most with spring – like sweetly scented jonquils and comely white tulips. The rich desserts of winter make way for lighter textures and tastes. Instead of delicious dark chocolate mousses, I opt for a creamy white chocolate mixture tingling with zesty lemon. To continue the lemon theme, I suggest serving this with confit *of lemon slices. The mousse can be served scooped into quenelles, or set in pretty ramekins or elegant wine glasses. I leave the portion size to you – it's often nicer to serve small portions of a mousse after a good dinner. Less is more enjoyable, I always say. Note that this contains lightly cooked eggs.*

SERVES 4–6

8 ounces white chocolate, broken in pieces
3 extra large egg yolks
¹/₂ cup confectioners' sugar
Grated zest of 1 lemon
2 cups heavy cream
Confit of Orange and Lemon (page 215, but made using
   all lemon slices instead of orange and lemon)

1 Melt the chocolate in a heatproof bowl set over a pan of barely simmering water. (We cover the bowl with plastic wrap, but you may prefer to put a plate on top.) Alternatively, you can melt the chocolate in the microwave, on a low heat. Take care when melting though, as white chocolate can "seize" more quickly than dark, because of its lack of cocoa solids. When melted, stir and cool.

2 Whisk the egg yolks and sugar in another heatproof bowl set over the same saucepan of simmering water. You will need to make a firm sabayon foam, so an electric mixer will help. The mixture is ready when you can swirl a foam trail that holds its shape on the surface. Remove from the pan of water and cool for 10 minutes, whisking once or twice.

3 Carefully fold the melted chocolate and lemon zest into the sabayon. Cool and then lightly chill, but make sure it doesn't set. It must still be quite soft when you add the cream.

4 Whip the cream until it holds soft peaks, then fold into the chocolate mixture, one third at a time, using a metal spatula. If serving in small dishes or glasses, divide the mousse among them. Chill until firm.

5 If serving as quenelles on dessert plates, place small spoonfuls of *confit* alongside. For ramekins or glasses, simply top each with a little *confit*.

Fresh Apple Parfait

This recipe is made in three stages – a creamy custard base, a meringue, and an apple cream – which are combined and then frozen. It is an ideal dinner party dessert. Be sure to use a good-quality apple cider. Or, if you have an electric juicer, you can crush your own juice using full-flavored Granny Smith or pippin apples. I use liquid glucose to stabilize the mixture; light corn syrup is an acceptable substitute. Note that this contains lightly cooked egg yolks and raw egg whites. SERVES **8**

1 quart apple cider or freshly pressed apple juice
4 egg yolks
1¼ cups superfine sugar
3 tablespoons light corn syrup
3 egg whites
1¼ cups heavy cream

1 Boil the cider until reduced to 1¼ cups. Remove from the heat, cool, and chill.

2 Heat a medium saucepan of water to boiling. Beat the egg yolks in a heatproof bowl that will fit over the saucepan. In another pan, heat ¾ cup of the sugar, the corn syrup, and ¼ cup water until on the point of boiling. Pour this gradually onto the yolks, whisking with a balloon whisk.

3 Set the bowl over the boiling water and turn the heat to medium. Cook, stirring frequently, until thickened. Remove and cool.

4 Beat the egg whites until softly stiff, then gradually beat in the remaining sugar until you have a firm and glossy meringue.

5 Whip the cream to firm, soft peaks, then whisk in the reduced apple cider.

6 Combine all three parts, folding together with a large metal spoon. Scoop into a long terrine mold of at least 2 pounds (8 cups) capacity, then freeze until solid.

7 To serve, thaw for 10 minutes, then cut into slices.

Note: A fresh green *jus* of Granny Smith apples would be a delicate accompaniment. Core 2 apples, then blend in a food processor with a squeeze of lemon juice. Strain, and trickle around each slice of parfait.

Rhubarb Cheesecake with Rhubarb Compote

At the beginning of spring, you can buy long, slender stems of tender rhubarb in a day-glo pink color. It needs little preparation except chopping into short lengths. Here it is pan-roasted and left to cool to a butterscotch-flavored compote. This is spooned on top of a light cheesecake mousse set on a crisp crumb base (we use English "digestive biscuits," but graham crackers are fine too). In the restaurant, we set this as baby cheesecakes in special deep molds, lining the sides with thin bâtons of peeled rhubarb first blanched in hot stock syrup. The cheesecake here is a simpler version, but is just as delicious. SERVES 6

1 cup heavy cream, lightly whipped

8 ounces graham crackers (½ 1-pound package)

6 tablespoons unsalted butter

2 teaspoons clear honey

½ cup cream cheese

½ cup crème fraîche

3–4 tablespoons sugar

Grated zest of 1 lime

2 teaspoons lime juice

Compote

1 pound young pink rhubarb

4 tablespoons unsalted butter

½ cup sugar

1 vanilla bean, slit open down the center

Sprigs fresh mint for decoration (optional)

1 First, make the compote. Rinse the rhubarb, pat dry, and trim off the base of the stems. Chop the rest into 1½-inch lengths.

2 Heat the butter in a non-stick frying pan and, when hot, quickly toss in the rhubarb pieces. Stir in the sugar and cook for about 5 minutes over a gentle heat until the rhubarb feels tender when pierced, but still keeps a good shape.

3 Meanwhile, scrape the seeds from the slit vanilla bean and mix with the heavy cream for the cheesecake. Set aside. Add the bean "shell" to the rhubarb compote, then leave it to cool and take on a vanilla flavor. Chill.

4 Crush the graham crackers to fine crumbs in a food processor. Or, place in a thick plastic bag, twist the top to seal, and gently bash with a rolling pin to crumbs. Don't wallop it too hard or the bag might burst. You should have about 3 cups.

5 Melt the butter with the honey in a saucepan, tip in the crumbs, and stir well until evenly mixed. Shake the mixture into a 9-inch springform cake pan. Pat down the crumbs to compress, using the back of a spoon, and press well up the sides. Chill until firm.

6 Blend the cream cheese, crème fraîche, and sugar with the lime zest and juice in a food processor until creamy. Scoop out into a mixing bowl. Whip the vanilla-flavored cream until softly stiff – that is, the cream forms soft peaks. Take care not to overwhip. Fold the cream into the cheese mixture and spoon onto the prepared crumb crust. Chill to firm.

7 Spoon the compote over the cheesecake just as you are about to serve, removing the vanilla bean beforehand. Alternatively, you can put a spoonful of compote on each plate next to a slice of cheesecake and decorate with mint sprigs.

summer

For me, summer begins mid-May. In fact, by the third week of May I'm well into the swing, because we are located next to the Chelsea Flower Show in London, and that, as every devotee of the social scene will tell you, is very definitely the start of the summer season here. Lunch during Chelsea week is unbelievably manic, but we are graced with some very elegant guests – and lovely hats!

Let's start with **tomatoes**, which are full of tremendous flavor from all the early summer heat. We use mainly plum tomatoes (the best come from Italy) and home-grown cherry tomatoes on the vine. We like to stuff plum tomatoes with a minced ratatouille to serve alongside grilled fish such as red mullet or pan-fried "cannons" of baby lamb. As a young *commis* chef in Paris, I remember being astounded by one of Guy Savoy's appetizers – plum tomato halves filled with shredded braised oxtail and then gratinéed. It was perfection, the sharp, fruity tomato cutting through the richness of the oxtail.

Cherry tomatoes have made a great difference to our cooking. Not only do they have an excellent flavor, but also the wonderful red of their skins means we seldom have to add any tomato paste to a stock or stew to pump up the color. Cherry tomatoes make great soups, delicious with thin floats of mozzarella *di bufala*, as well as a punchy gazpacho sauce and a tomato vinaigrette.

For a clever garnish, you might want to try making tomato *tuiles* or "chips." It's really easy, but you do need to use an oven that has a very low setting – almost a plate-warming temperature. Failing that, you can prop open the oven door with a wooden spoon. All you do is thinly slice very firm, bright red plum or beef tomatoes with a serrated knife, lay the slices on a non-stick cooking liner on a baking sheet, and sprinkle with sea salt and black pepper. Then simply dry out in the low oven for a good few hours until the tomatoes are firm and you can peel them off the liner. Timing depends on your oven. In ours, it takes 12–16 hours on a pilot light (few domestic ovens have such things now). The first time you make them, start them in the morning and check after 4 hours, then thereafter every hour or so. Once they are dry, lay them on a wire rack to cool and crisp further.

Around Chelsea time we start to get in supplies of my favorite summer food, the kidney-shaped **Jersey Royal new potatoes**. I could happily sit and eat a bowl of them on their own, as they have so much flavor. From a cook's point of view, you can really do a lot with them because of their waxy texture. They make a good *pomme purée*, using the larger sizes – bake them on a bed of rock salt (to maintain the waxiness), peel while still warm (wearing rubber gloves), and then put through a potato ricer. We also crush boiled Jerseys against the side of a pan and mix in olive oil, chopped olives, and tomatoes, to make *pommes écrasées*. And they are brilliant sautéed in olive oil or goose fat. The skins of Jersey Royals are so delicate that they only need to be lightly scrubbed if serving whole – plain boiled or warm in salads (for the simplest, just toss them while still hot in some vinaigrette). A great potato salad is Jerseys mixed with a little homemade mayonnaise (thinned down slightly with cream or more vinaigrette) and chopped green onions and topped with chopped fresh parsley or chervil. Jersey Royals have such a short season – about six to eight weeks (they can't be grown anywhere other than Jersey, one of the islands in the English Channel) – so we really make the most of them.

I don't know who first had the brilliant idea to try cooking with **squash flowers**, but I am grateful for the source of inspiration. As an ingredient, they are truly versatile, with an enchanting fragile beauty. We are supplied flowers with tiny wee vegetables, the length of my little finger, still attached. I know you cannot buy them easily, but home gardeners will find them simple to grow, so squash flowers need not be thought of as elitist. In France, specialty growers insert thin plastic cups into the emerging flowers so the petals grow into a cup shape. This makes the mature flower the perfect shape for stuffing.

I use squash flowers in two ways, always with the baby vegetable still attached. For the first, the flowers are filled with a light *farci* or stuffing, such as a mousse, a minced ratatouille, or even a spicy couscous, and then steamed over an aromatic simmering stock. I serve them with a delicate *jus* of Jerusalem artichokes

Even in summer, many of our clients enjoy a nice piece of steak, often with a light sauce such as creamed parsley purée and sautéed chanterelles. A favorite cut of mine is a boneless beef **steak** from the short loin (on the bone it is the classic T-bone steak). It is just as good as a filet mignon for tenderness with, I think, more flavor. It takes just minutes to cook. We buy short-loin steak in a large piece, wrap it tightly in plastic wrap, and refrigerate for 24 hours to "set" the shape, before cutting into even-size steaks.

Summer isn't summer without **peaches**. My favorite ones are the white-flesh varieties from Italy, which reach our suppliers from May onward. Later on, firm and juicy yellow peaches appear. While there is little to beat a perfect fresh peach served simply sliced, peaches are a very versatile ingredient and we capitalize on this in our kitchen, for both sweet and savory dishes. At the height of gluts, we make jars of peach chutney (see the recipe on page 213) to serve as a relish with fresh foie gras, pâté, and butter-roasted chicken, and with cheese and walnut bread. Pan-fried peaches glazed with sugar and vinegar are memorable with duck, goose, or lamb.

One of my favorite ways of serving peaches is to marry the sweet, succulent flesh with aromatic thyme, an herb that seems to cut the richness of the peach flavor and heighten the fruitiness. It's a combination that works well for peaches simply poached in a thyme-flavored sugar syrup and for peaches served with homemade thyme ice cream.

We also make light, crisp peach *tuiles*, by slicing just ripe and firm fruit wafer-thin, brushing with stock syrup, and oven-drying for a few hours. To get the roof-tile shape, we press the dried slices over a rolling pin and leave them to crisp. Peach *tuiles* are a very pretty garnish for creamy puddings.

In mid- to late summer our supplies of **figs** come in from Italy. These beautiful plump, dark-skinned fruits with a downy surface and pert little hooked tips have quite a short season, so we use them every way we can. You have to judge the ripeness fairly exactly. If underripe, they leak a white milkiness; if too ripe, they become squashy. I love to roast them whole with a balsamic-flavored caramel or simply with sugar, butter, and cinnamon. They can be simmered into a chunky chutney, delicious with foie gras. We also slice firm fruits wafer-thin and dry them as *tuiles*. My latest creation is fig *carpaccio*, which is embarrassingly simple to make. Take firm fruit and peel thinly, removing the tips, then cut in half and scoop out the seeds. Lay the halves between large sheets of plastic wrap and bat with a rolling pin until very thin. Don't whack too hard, just enough to flatten thinly and evenly. Then freeze and keep like this until ready to serve. Remove from the freezer, peel off the plastic wrap, and place directly on a large, flat dinner plate. Top with a coarse pâté, like the Mosaic of Autumn Game on page 130, or some heavenly slices of pan-fried foie gras. What more can I say?

In the early days of the Aubergine restaurant, we were very daring and gave our guests ripe fresh **cherries** nestled in bowls of crushed ice instead of petits fours. The idea went down a storm, as the juicy fruitiness cleared satiated palates perfectly. At the height of summer, we get luscious dark red cherries from Spain, and I really enjoy working my way through a pile of them. At other times of the year, growers in Italy, America, Chile, and South Africa fly us in beautifully sweet fruits. Cherries are good in both sweet and savory dishes. They make a classic partnership with duck breasts, and I like them with caramel and balsamic sauce. You can use them in a dessert soup, too, as well as for fresh cherry ice cream (pit and crush 2½–3 cups cherries, then blend with a rich crème anglaise and churn in an ice cream machine). Great with almondy cookies.

I know **chocolate** is not a seasonal food, but I associate it with summer, because I like to combine it with the heady fragrance of lavender flowers. I was introduced to the idea of combining chocolate and lavender by a talented French *chocolatier* whom I met while cooking as a guest chef at the Singapore Raffles. Such a "marriage" of flavors isn't really surprising, of course – from the early days of chocolate-making in Europe, cooks have enhanced chocolate with flowery flavors. Examples are rose, as found in chocolate-coated Turkish delight bars, and violet, geranium, and other flower creams in chocolate boxes. Dark, milk, and white chocolate all benefit from the lavender connection. With white chocolate, we like to melt the chocolate slowly, even overnight, over a warm hot cupboard, with a healthy-sized sprig or two of lavender flowerheads to give their perfume. The next day the lavender is strained or spooned out, leaving its flowery fragrance in the chocolate.

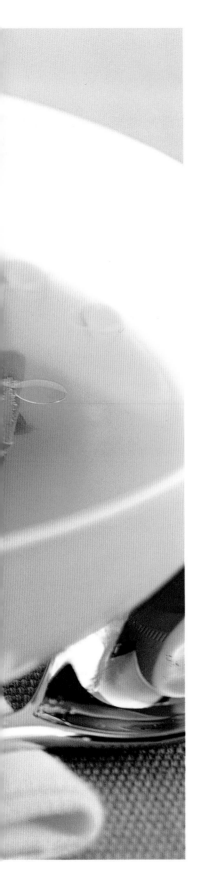

Light Tomato Broth with a Paysanne of Vegetables

This is a version of a tomato consommé we serve in the restaurant with baby lobster tails. As a chilled summer soup it is unsurpassed. I guarantee you will not taste such a full, fresh tomato flavor anywhere, yet it looks as clear and bright as a glass of sparkling wine. The floating garnish flaunts the choicest summer vegetables. **SERVES 4 AS A FIRST COURSE**

2 large shallots, chopped

¼ cup olive oil, plus extra for serving

2¼ pounds ripe plum tomatoes, roughly chopped

2 cloves garlic, sliced

1 teaspoon fine sea salt

1 teaspoon sugar

1 teaspoon each chopped fresh basil, chervil, and tarragon

4 egg whites

¼ teaspoon each white peppercorns and black peppercorns

2 ounces snow peas, trimmed

2 ounces fine green beans, trimmed

About 20 asparagus tips

1 Sweat the shallots in 3 tablespoons of the oil for 3 minutes until softened, then stir in three-fourths of the chopped tomatoes, the garlic, sea salt, sugar, and herbs. Cook over medium heat for about 10 minutes, stirring occasionally, until a little pulpy.

2 Pour in 4 cups water and bring to a boil. Simmer for about 20 minutes, skimming the surface with a large spoon to remove any froth.

3 Line a colander with a large, wet piece of cheesecloth or thin, clean dish towel and set over a bowl. Pour the tomato liquid through the colander, pressing down on the debris with the back of a ladle. Chill the liquid by standing the bowl in a larger bowl of ice water.

4 Blend the remaining chopped tomatoes with the egg whites and peppercorns in a food processor. Tip into a large saucepan and add the strained tomato liquid.

5 Bring the contents of the pan slowly to a boil and simmer for 20 minutes. You should notice the liquid becoming crystal clear as it bubbles.

6 Rinse out the cheesecloth or dish towel and place back in the colander set over a bowl. Slowly pour the liquid into the lined colander – it should run through beautifully clear. If it does not, slowly pour it back through the colander set over another bowl. Chill until ready to serve.

7 To make the garnish, cut the snow peas in diamonds. Heat the remaining tablespoon of oil in a small frying pan and gently fry the snow peas, beans, and asparagus tips for about 3 minutes until just wilted. Drain on paper towels.

8 Scatter the snow peas, beans, and asparagus into four large soup bowls. Pour the clear broth over. If you like, you can drizzle with extra virgin olive oil, then serve.

Pepper and Tomato Soup with Crab Cocktail

A soup does not have to be brimming with liquid and a miscellany of floating diced solids. Sometimes I like to create a centerpiece of a mixture like this seafood cocktail and surround it with a light, flavorsome broth. Choose ripe plum tomatoes for this recipe. If you wish to give the pepper more kick, broil or roast it first. Fresh crab is best, as it is less watery than frozen and has a sweeter flavor than canned. In the colder winter months you could use lobster meat instead of crab. SERVES **4** AS A FIRST COURSE

3 tablespoons olive oil, plus
   extra for drizzling
2 large red sweet peppers, about 1 pound
   total weight, chopped
6 large, ripe plum tomatoes, about 1 pound
   total weight, chopped
4 shallots, chopped
About 12 leaves fresh basil
1 sprig fresh thyme
1 small bay leaf
3$\frac{1}{3}$ cups tomato juice
$\frac{1}{2}$ cup heavy cream
8 ounces fresh white crab meat (about 2 cups)

1 Granny Smith apple, peeled, cored,
   and finely diced
1 very small head romaine lettuce,
   finely shredded
1 ripe avocado
Sea salt and freshly ground black pepper

Sauce
4–6 tablespoons Mayonnaise (page 213)
1 tablespoon tomato paste
A few drops of hot pepper sauce
Juice of 1 lime

1 Heat the oil in a large saucepan, then add the peppers, tomatoes, shallots, and herbs. Sauté gently for about 5 minutes, then stir, cover, and leave to cook gently for 10 minutes.
2 Uncover, and remove the thyme and bay leaf. Stir in the tomato juice and cream, season well, and allow to cool. Blend in a food processor or blender until smooth and creamy, scraping down the sides once or twice. Rub through a sieve into a bowl, using the back of a ladle. Chill the soup for at least 2 hours.
3 Meanwhile, check the crab with a fork for any flecks of shell and cartilage, which can be so irritating to bite on in the middle of a dream dish. Put in a bowl with the apple and lettuce.
4 For the sauce, beat the mayonnaise with the tomato paste, pepper sauce, half the lime juice, and some seasoning. Mix just enough into the crab to make a nice firm but moist mixture.
5 Crush the avocado with a fork. Add the remaining lime juice and some seasoning.
6 Check the soup for seasoning. (Chilled foods need more seasoning than hot ones.)
7 Set a plain biscuit cutter, about 2 inches in diameter, in the middle of a wide soup bowl. Spoon one-fourth of the avocado into the base of the cutter, then add one-fourth of the crab mix over that. (See photographs of this technique on page 221.) Finally, coat the top of the crab with a little of the remaining cocktail sauce, and carefully lift off the cutter. Repeat with three more soup bowls.
8 Pour the soup around each crab cocktail, add a drizzle of oil if you like, and serve immediately.

Lobster with Mango and Spinach Salad

This dish is a real treat for the eye – simply stunning colors of pink, gold, and deep green.
I would advise that for the best flavor you cook your own lobsters (put them in the freezer first to
make them sleepy). Another useful hint is that it is easier to shell them while they are still warm.

SERVES 4 AS A FIRST COURSE OR LIGHT DISH

Court Bouillon (page 212)
4 small live lobsters, about 1½ pounds each
2 just ripe mangoes
3 tablespoons Classic Vinaigrette (page 213)
5 ounces baby spinach leaves (about 1½ cups)
Sea salt and freshly ground black pepper

1 Bring the court bouillon to a gentle boil, then drop in the lobsters. Poach them for
5–6 minutes. Remove the pan from the heat and allow the lobsters to cool a little in the bouillon.
2 When the lobsters are cool enough for you to handle (wear rubber gloves), remove them and
take the meat from the shells. Use strong kitchen scissors or poultry shears to cut through the
body shell, and take out the meat in one piece. Check the third disk along for the dirt sac and
pull this out. Extract the meat from the claws and knuckles by cracking the shells with the back
of the knife. Chop the claw and knuckle meat. Put all the shelled meat back into the bouillon and
leave to cool down and absorb more flavor. When cold, remove and drain.
3 Peel the mangoes, cut the flesh off the central pit, and chop into small dice. Toss with
half the vinaigrette.
4 Toss the spinach leaves in the remaining vinaigrette and season well. Arrange the spinach
in the center of four plates (we arrange ours in a petal pattern).
5 Scatter the dressed mango over. Put the lobster knuckle and claw meat in the center.
Slice the lobster tail meat and arrange on top of the mango. Serve.

Salad of Bay Scallops, Baby Calamari, and Confit New Potatoes

Dainty, pretty, and in a class of its own, this is an elegant first course for a special summer dinner. You need the very small baby calamari (squid), sold as cleaned tubes with the tentacles pushed inside and the tiny bite-size bay scallops. If possible, buy fresh scallops, not frozen, or the flesh may be watery. The goose fat for the confit *potatoes can be bought in cans.*

SERVES 4 AS A FIRST COURSE

8 ounces baby new potatoes
  (the smaller the better)
½ cup goose fat
1 cup tepid milk
Scant 1 cup all-purpose flour
1 teaspoon rapid-rise active dry yeast
4 baby calamari (squid), about
  3 ounces each
About 32–40 bay scallops,
  shucked

⅛ teaspoon mild curry powder
Light olive oil for frying
4–6 tablespoons Classic Vinaigrette (page 213)
  mixed with 2 teaspoons chopped fresh tarragon
About 10 ounces mixed salad leaves (varieties
  with soft leaves such as mâche or oak leaf)
Sea salt and freshly ground black pepper

1 First, *confit* the potatoes, which has to be done on a very low heat. You may find a metal heat diffuser useful. Put the potatoes and goose fat into a small saucepan – the potatoes should be covered in the fat. Cook on the lowest heat setting for 20–25 minutes until just tender. The fat may bubble occasionally, but don't let it get any hotter. The potatoes should cook, not fry. Drain on paper towels and cool. Save the fat.

2 Blend the milk, flour, yeast, and a large pinch of salt to a thick batter in a food processor or blender. Tip into a shallow bowl and set aside in the fridge for 1 hour.

3 Check the calamari are clean inside, then pat dry.

4 Season the scallops with a little salt, pepper, and curry powder to coat. Heat 1 tablespoon of oil in a frying pan and, when hot, add the scallops and quickly toss for less than a minute. Remove and drain, then toss in half the vinaigrette. Set aside.

5 Halve the new potatoes. Heat a tablespoon of the saved goose fat in a frying pan. When hot, quickly brown the potatoes until crisp, then drain and season. Keep warm.

6 Pick over the salad leaves, season, and toss with the remaining vinaigrette. Mound in the center of four large plates.

7 Heat about ½ inch of oil in a frying pan. Remove the batter from the fridge and dip in the calamari bodies and tentacles, coating evenly. Lay them in the hot oil and cook for a couple of minutes on each side until crisp and golden. Do not overcook. Drain and season.

8 Spoon the scallops on top of the salad and sit the calamari on top of that. Arrange the potatoes around the salad and serve.

Tartare of Scallops and Golden Caviar with Tomato Jus

Because our scallops are so fresh, they are perfect for delicate and creamy tartares, *which are simple and pure in flavor. However, when gently blended with a spoonful of the rare Imperial caviar they become exquisite. Imperial caviar (a.k.a. golden Osietra), the roe of the albino Caraburun sturgeon, is a brilliant gold color with a mild, almost nutty flavor. My occasional supply comes from Imperial Caviar UK in 50-g cans. Use half in the* tartare *and the rest delicately balanced on top as a glistening garnish. The* jus *served around the* tartare *is made from the extract of fresh tomatoes left to drip overnight – suprisingly it is clear and gives no indication of the food origin until you sip it. Quite, quite clever, I think.* **SERVES 4 AS A FIRST COURSE**

1 pound ripe plum tomatoes
2 large leaves fresh basil
8 very fresh sea scallops, shucked,
 without corals
1 tablespoon crème fraîche
1 tablespoon mascarpone
1 teaspoon chopped fresh chervil
1 teaspoon chopped fresh chives
Juice of ½ lime (approximately)
50 g (2 ounces) Imperial caviar
Sea salt

1 First, make the tomato *jus*. Chop the tomatoes roughly, then blend in a food processor with the basil and a little salt for just a few seconds to a chunky purée. Tip into a clean jelly bag that is held suspended above a bowl. Allow the juice to drip through overnight. The liquid will run clear.
2 Now, if you wish, you could boil the juice down to reduce it by half and concentrate the flavor, but then it won't taste as fresh. Chill the *jus*.
3 For the *tartare*, mince the scallops very, very finely by hand, then mix with the crème fraîche, mascarpone, herbs, and salt. Drop by drop, add lime juice, tasting as you go, until you feel it's sufficient. Gently fold in half the caviar.
4 Place a 2-inch plain biscuit cutter in the middle of a small shallow bowl. Spoon in one-fourth of the *tartare* and level the top lightly. Lift off the cutter, and repeat with three other bowls.
5 Spoon the remaining caviar on top of each *tartare* as a garnish. Serve lightly chilled, with the tomato *jus* in a separate little pitcher to drizzle around the mounds.

Summery Quails in a Tomato and Tarragon Dressing

Quails look so inviting with their small plump breasts. Many people find them fiddly to eat, so we remove the breasts after roasting and cool them in a light tomato dressing. They are served on a warm salad of celery and chanterelles. A terrific dish. **SERVES 4 AS A FIRST COURSE**

4 fresh quails

6 tablespoons olive oil

½ small tomato, seeded
  and very finely minced

½ shallot, very finely minced

½ teaspoon tomato ketchup

½ teaspoon coarsegrain mustard

½ teaspoon fresh lemon juice

1 teaspoon chopped fresh tarragon

4 small stalks celery, cut into small lengths

½ cup Chicken Stock (page 212)
  or Vegetable *Nage* (page 212)

3 ounces fresh chanterelles, ends trimmed,
  then halved if large

A few celery leaves for garnish
  (can be deep-fried, if liked)

Sea salt and freshly ground black pepper

1 Preheat the oven to 375°. Brush the quails lightly with a little of the oil, season, and roast for 12 minutes.

2 Meanwhile, make a dressing by mixing together the minced tomato, shallot, ketchup, mustard, lemon juice, tarragon, and 3 tablespoons of the oil. Season well.

3 Remove the quails from the oven and allow to stand for 10 minutes. Using a sharp boning knife, remove the lightly cooked breasts, keeping them whole. (Use the carcasses in a stock.) Mix the breasts into the tomato dressing and set aside to cool.

4 Heat 1 tablespoon of the remaining oil in a small frying pan and sauté the celery until golden brown. Pour in the stock or *nage*, season nicely, and cover the celery with a butter wrapper. Simmer for about 10 minutes until softened and the liquid has evaporated away.

5 Meanwhile, sauté the chanterelles in the last of the oil for about 5 minutes, stirring once or twice, then season.

6 To serve, place the celery in the center of four dinner plates. Spoon the chanterelles on top. Arrange the quail breasts on top of that and trickle any leftover dressing around. Garnish with celery leaves.

Linguine in Lobster and Chanterelle Sauce

This is something of a classic dish (with sauce américaine), and you will need time and patience to make it. But it is certainly worth it. It is best to buy live lobster for this dish, as you need to sauté the shells to give a good color to the sauce. Buy the linguine fresh if you can, from a good Italian store. **SERVES 4 AS A FIRST COURSE**

2 live lobsters, about 1½ pounds each
A little olive oil for frying
1 small carrot, finely diced
1 small leek, finely diced
1 small onion, minced
1 small stalk celery, finely diced
2 tablespoons Pernod
½ cup dry white wine
1 medium tomato, chopped
2 teaspoons tomato paste

2 cups Fish Stock (page 212)
   or Light Chicken Stock (page 212)
1 cup heavy cream
2 large leaves fresh basil
4 ounces fresh chanterelles, trimmed
2 tablespoons butter
Leaves from a small bunch of fresh
   flat-leaf parsley, chopped
10 ounces fresh linguine
Sea salt and freshly ground black pepper

1 First, prepare the lobsters. Freeze them for 30 minutes so they become sleepy. Bring a large pan of water to a boil and drop in the lobsters. Leave for a minute, then remove from the water and cool until you can handle them. Pull off the head and claws. Extract the meat from the body shell using sharp scissors or poultry shears to cut through. The meat will still be raw, but sufficiently loosened for you to pull it out. Extract the meat from the claws. Set the meat aside.

2 Smash the lobster shells a bit so they will fit into a large pan. Heat 2–3 tablespoons of oil in the pan and sauté the shells until bright pink. Stir in the carrot, leek, and onion, and cook these for about 10 minutes until nicely caramelized. Stir in the Pernod and cook until it evaporates, then add the wine and cook until syrupy. Add the tomato and tomato paste. Cook for a further 5 minutes until the pan contents look quite sticky. Pour in the stock and boil until it reduces down by half. Finally, add the cream and basil leaves. Remove the pan from the heat and allow to cool, occasionally mashing the shells with a large ladle to extract as much flavor as possible. Strain through a sieve into a smaller pan ready for reheating.

3 Heat a dry heavy-based pan and sauté the chanterelles to draw out the moisture. Drain on paper towels, and pour away the liquid from the pan. Heat the butter in the pan and, when it stops foaming, sauté the chanterelles quickly until nicely cooked. Season and sprinkle with a little chopped parsley. Keep warm.

4 Cook the linguine in boiling salted water until *al dente*, 2–3 minutes. Drain and mix with a couple of spoonfuls of the sauce. Keep hot.

5 Heat another frying pan with a little oil and sauté the lobster meat for 2–3 minutes. Slice the tail meat into medallions and season.

6 Reheat the remaining sauce. Serve the linguine in the center of four warmed plates. Place lobster and chanterelles on top, spoon the sauce over, and sprinkle with the last of the parsley.

Poached Wild Salmon with Gewürtztraminer Sauce

Wild salmon has a leaner texture, darker color, and finer flavor than farmed salmon, purely because it grows in a totally natural ocean environment – swimming in strong currents and feeding on a completely wild diet. A rich fish, salmon suits sweet wine sauces, especially the spicy Gewürtztraminer wine. Serve with blanched and buttery wild asparagus and an accompaniment of baby new potatoes and broccoli florets in an almondy-butter dressing.

SERVES 4 AS A MAIN DISH

4 *darnes* of wild salmon (steaks from
   the middle of the fish with a central
   bone and skin), about 5 ounces each
Court Bouillon (page 212) for poaching
4 ounces wild or thin asparagus spears
A little melted butter
Sea salt and freshly ground black pepper

Sauce
1¼ cups Gewürtztraminer wine
1¼ cups Fish Stock (page 212)
3 tablespoons heavy cream
2 tablespoons butter

1 Make sure the salmon is clean and free of any blood in the cavity region. Bring the court bouillon to a gentle boil, then slip in the *darnes*. Remove from the heat and leave the fish to cook in the residual heat for 10 minutes.

2 Meanwhile, to make the sauce, boil the wine and stock together until reduced down by half to 1¼ cups. Whisk in the cream and butter, and check the seasoning.

3 Blanch the asparagus in boiling water for 2 minutes, then drain and refresh in ice water. Drain again, then place in a small saucepan with a little melted butter ready for reheating.

4 Remove the fish from the bouillon when it feels firm. Carefully pull out the central bones and gently peel away the skin. Lay the *darnes* on warmed dinner plates.

5 Briefly reheat the asparagus in the melted butter, then place over the salmon. Spoon a little sauce over and strain the rest into a sauceboat to pass around separately.

Wild Salmon with Wilted Lettuce and Cucumber Salad and a Vine-Tomato Butter Sauce

The wild salmon season runs through the summer months. Out of season, the next best salmon is that farmed or ranched on a near natural (organic) diet, with artificial currents to encourage them to develop muscle. The salad and sauce here are Mediterranean-inspired.

SERVES 4 AS A MAIN DISH

4 thick-cut fillets of wild salmon,
   about 5 ounces each, skinned
3 tablespoons olive oil
1 large English cucumber, peeled and diced
2 tomatoes, skinned, seeded, and chopped
²/₃ cup black olives, pitted and chopped
1 tablespoon chopped fresh parsley
2 baby heads romaine lettuce
3 tablespoons Classic Vinaigrette (page 213)
Sea salt and freshly ground black pepper

Sauce
8 ounces vine-ripened tomatoes
1 teaspoon sherry vinegar
1 teaspoon sugar
1 tablespoon chopped fresh basil
½ cup heavy cream
4 tablespoons butter, diced

1 Rub both sides of the fillets with 1 tablespoon of the olive oil and set aside.

2 Mix together the cucumber, tomatoes, olives, and parsley. Season well and set this salad aside.

3 Make the sauce: Halve the tomatoes and blend with the vinegar, sugar, and basil in a food processor. Pour through a sieve into a saucepan, rubbing with the back of a ladle. Cook, uncovered, for about 10 minutes until reduced by half. Mix in the cream and simmer for a minute or two, then whisk in the diced butter until nice and smooth. Season and set aside.

4 Divide the lettuce into leaves, discarding the core. Heat the remaining oil and sauté the leaves for about 2 minutes until wilted. Season and set aside.

5 Heat a heavy-based, non-stick frying pan and, when hot, add the salmon, skinned side down. Turn the heat to medium and cook for 3–4 minutes. Season the fish as it cooks. Turn over carefully and cook the other side for 2–3 minutes until the fish feels lightly springy. Season again.

6 To serve, dress the salad with the vinaigrette and place in the center of four dinner plates. (In the restaurant we mold it neatly in a plain biscuit cutter.) Arrange the wilted lettuce on top and then the salmon. Drizzle the sauce around.

Trout with a Lemon and Caviar Sabayon

I adore fishing, and sneak out to beaches or river banks whenever I can. From May to August is the mayfly season in England, so I head down to the river Kennet and cast my line with a mayfly bait (sprayed with oil to help it float). When I land brown trout, this is how I like to cook and serve them at home, with a classically simple, light and eggy sabayon flavored with lemon and a spoon of Osietra caviar. The preparation suits other trout, such as brook and steelhead, too. Baby new potatoes and fresh peas are the best accompaniments. SERVES 4 AS A MAIN DISH

2 trout (preferably wild), about
  2¼ pounds each
2 large globe artichokes
A squeeze of lemon juice
A little olive oil for frying
1 tablespoon butter
Sea salt and freshly ground black pepper

Sabayon
6 egg yolks
1 teaspoon lemon juice
Grated zest of 1 small lemon
1 tablespoon Osietra caviar

1 Fillet the trouts, leaving the skin on. (Or ask your fish merchant to do this.) Check the flesh for pinbones with your fingertips and pull out with tweezers or thin pliers. Score the skin several times in even cuts using the tip of a razor-sharp knife. Set aside.

2 Cut off the artichoke stalks, pull off the leaves, trim the bases, and cut out the hairy choke, to leave the bottoms. (See photographs of this technique on page 216.) Cook the bottoms in boiling salted water with a good squeeze of lemon juice for about 15 minutes. Drain and cool, then cut into diamonds or slices.

3 Fry the pieces of artichoke in a little oil and butter until nicely browned. Drain and keep warm.

4 Preheat the broiler. Meanwhile, make the sabayon. Whisk the yolks, lemon juice, 1 tablespoon water, and seasoning in a bowl set over a pan of simmering water until the mixture triples in volume and becomes light and frothy. (It is best to do this with a portable electric mixer.) Remove the bowl from the water and set aside while you cook the trout.

5 Brush the trout skin with a little oil and broil for about 4 minutes to crisp the skin. Turn over, season the flesh, and brush with more oil. Return to the broiler and cook for a few more minutes until just browned. Move farther away from the heat, and continue cooking until the trout feels just firm but still springy when pressed, 4–5 more minutes.

6 Return the bowl of sabayon to the simmering water and whisk quickly to froth up. Then off the heat, fold in the lemon zest and caviar.

7 Transfer the fish to four warmed plates, arrange the artichoke pieces around, and spoon the sauce over the top. Serve immediately.

Turbot with Squash Flower Fritters and Noilly Prat Sauce

When squash flowers are in season, I like to dip them in a light beer batter and fry them, holding them down with a spatula in the hot oil so they cook flat. These go on top of fillets of turbot, served on a bed of wilted spinach with a Noilly Prat velouté. **SERVES 4 AS A MAIN DISH**

4 zucchini flowers, still with
   tiny whole zucchini attached
$\frac{1}{2}$ cup tepid milk
$\frac{1}{2}$ cup all-purpose flour, plus extra for dusting
1 teaspoon rapid-rise active dry yeast
1 teaspoon beer
1 medium zucchini, cut into small even dice
Light olive oil for frying
4 fillets of turbot, about 4 ounces each,
   skinned (ideally cut in *tranche* shapes)
1 tablespoon butter
1 cup Fish Stock (page 212)
4 ounces baby leaf spinach (about 1 cup)

Sauce
2 shallots, chopped
2 teaspoons butter
$\frac{1}{2}$ cup dry white wine
$\frac{1}{2}$ cup Noilly Prat vermouth
1 cup Fish Stock (page 212)
1 teaspoon chopped fresh tarragon
Scant 1 cup heavy cream
A squeeze of lemon juice
Sea salt and freshly ground black
   pepper

1 First, make the sauce. Sauté the shallots in the butter for 5 minutes until softened. Pour in the wine and Noilly Prat and cook until reduced to a syrupy consistency. Add the fish stock and tarragon. Boil until reduced by half. Add the cream and boil until reduced by half again. Check the seasoning, add a squeeze of lemon juice, and pass through a sieve into a clean pan. Set aside.

2 Now, for the flowers. Split the tiny zucchini (still attached to the flowers) up the middle. Whisk the milk with the flour, yeast, beer, and a large pinch of salt. Set aside.

3 Lightly sauté the diced zucchini in a little hot oil until lightly colored. Season and drain on a paper towel. Preheat the oven to 400°.

4 Heat a tablespoon of oil in a non-stick frying pan (with an ovenproof handle) and, when hot, fry the turbot until it caramelizes nicely on one side. Slide in the butter and carefully flip the fish over. Pour in the fish stock. Cover with a butter wrapper and transfer to the oven to cook for about 7 minutes, basting once with the stock. Remove the fish and allow to stand.

5 Now back to the zucchini flowers. Toss them with a little flour. Heat $\frac{3}{4}$-inch depth of oil in a deep frying pan to about 350°. When it is hot, dip a flower into the batter, press open the tiny zucchini, and slip it gently into the hot oil. Using a metal spatula, hold the zucchini open if possible so it cooks flat. Cook for a minute or two until golden brown, then remove and drain. Repeat with the other flowers.

6 To serve, make sure your plates are very hot, and press the spinach leaves into the center of each, so they wilt. Drain the turbot and put a fillet on each mound of spinach. Reheat the diced zucchini in a small pan and sprinkle over. Reheat the sauce and coat the fish with a little; serve the rest separately in a small pitcher. Finally, top the fish with the crisp-fried zucchini flowers.

Fricassee of Scallops and Chanterelles with Lettuce Sauce

Chanterelles, or girolles, the little, golden, fairy-like mushrooms with a divine flavor, are one of the culinary delights of summer. They need to be trimmed at the stem end, but after that is done this is quite a quick dish to put together. (Out of season, you may like to use dried chanterelles, which can be restored by soaking and then patting dry.) Make sure the scallops you use are plump sea scallops – mine are hand-dived in cold Scottish waters. The sauce is unusual, a light cream of lettuce. In the restaurant we also garnish this with whole garlic cloves confit *in goose fat and then fried until the skins become crisp. An ideal dish for a light summery lunch.*

SERVES 4 AS A LIGHT DISH OR 6 AS A FIRST COURSE

10 ounces small fresh chanterelles
1 head romaine lettuce, shredded
1 clove garlic, peeled and left whole
1/3 cup chopped Canadian bacon
4 green onions, chopped
4–6 tablespoons olive oil
1/2 cup Classic Vinaigrette (page 213)
Juice of 1/2 small lemon

1 tablespoon chopped fresh chives,
   plus extra for sprinkling
1 tablespoon chopped fresh chervil,
   plus extra sprigs for garnish
6 sea scallops, shucked, without corals
1/2 teaspoon mild curry powder
Sea salt and freshly ground black pepper

1 Using a small sharp knife, trim the ends of the chanterelles. Set aside.

2 Make the sauce: Sauté the lettuce with the garlic clove, bacon, and one of the green onions in 1 tablespoon of the oil until wilted, 3–5 minutes. Remove the garlic clove and discard. Blend the lettuce, bacon, and onion plus any pan juices in a food processor, then pass through a sieve into another small pan, rubbing with the back of a ladle. Season, return the sauce to a simmer, and cook for 3 minutes to reduce down by about a third. Beat in the vinaigrette and set aside.

3 Heat a frying pan with 2 tablespoons of the oil and sauté the chanterelles and the rest of the green onions with the lemon juice, stirring occasionally, for about 3 minutes. Season and mix in the chopped herbs. Set aside and keep warm.

4 When you are ready to serve, heat the last of the oil in a frying pan. Add the scallops, arranging them in a circle. Season nicely and sprinkle the curry powder over. After 2 minutes, turn the scallops, in the same order you placed them in the pan, and cook the other side until nicely golden, 1–2 minutes. Season again. The scallops should feel quite bouncy when pressed lightly. Don't overcook them. Slice each in half horizontally.

5 To serve, spoon the chanterelle mixture in the center of four warmed plates and arrange the scallops on top. Spoon the sauce around and finish with a sprinkling of chives and a sprig or two of chervil.

Roasted Sea Bass with Chive Crème Fraîche, Baby Potatoes, and Artichokes

This dish is so simple and so fresh. Wild sea bass, reared and caught naturally, has a greater depth of flavor than farmed. It also has a firmer texture because the fish swim against tides and currents and so develop leaner muscle. Match it with other summer favorites – firm, waxy new potatoes and fresh artichokes or crisp green beans. **SERVES 4 AS A MAIN DISH**

2 large globe artichokes

1 tablespoon lemon juice

1 pound new potatoes

2 tablespoons chopped fresh chives

½ cup thick crème fraîche

6 tablespoons olive oil

1 tablespoon shredded fresh basil

½ cup Classic Vinaigrette (page 213)

2 shallots, minced

1 tablespoon sherry vinegar

2 tablespoons heavy cream

1¾-pound fillet of sea bass, trimmed and cut into 4 neat portions, skin on

Sprigs fresh thyme for garnish

Sea salt and freshly ground black pepper

1 Cut off the artichoke stalks, pull off the leaves, and cut out the hairy chokes, leaving you with just the cup-shaped meaty bottoms (see photographs of this technique on page 216). Cut the bottoms into lengths and then into diamond shapes.

2 Cook the pieces of artichoke in boiling water with the lemon juice for 10 minutes until barely tender; drain. At the same time, boil the new potatoes in another pan until only just tender; drain when they are ready, then cut them in half.

3 Meanwhile, mix the chives into the crème fraîche and season nicely. Set aside.

4 Heat 2 tablespoons of the oil in a frying pan and sauté the potatoes for about 5 minutes until nicely colored. Remove with a slotted spoon and drain on a paper towel. Beat the basil into the vinaigrette, then mix with the warm potatoes and leave to cool.

5 Add the artichokes to the frying pan, with another tablespoon of oil if necessary, and sauté for 3–5 minutes until nicely colored. Remove with a draining spoon, drain, and keep warm.

6 Add the shallots to the pan and sauté for 5 minutes until softened. Deglaze with the vinegar and cook until the liquid has reduced away. Stir in the cream, season, and set aside to keep warm.

7 Score the skin of the bass several times with the tip of a very sharp knife. Heat the remaining oil in a large frying pan. Season the bass and cook, skin-side down, for 3–4 minutes until the silver skin is crisp. Turn carefully and cook the other side for 1–2 minutes until lightly springy when pressed. Season again.

8 To serve, spoon the artichokes in the center of four warmed plates. Spoon the shallot cream on top. Sit the sea bass on this, arrange the basil potatoes around the fish, and garnish with thyme. Finally, spoon the chive crème fraîche on top so it melts invitingly over the fish as you serve.

Sautéed Foie Gras with Peach Chutney

This is the ultimate quick snack, once you've made the chutney. Foie gras needs to be fresh, so order it from a reputable butcher. Follow the instructions carefully for preparing and cooking it, as it is too special to mess up. French chef Michel Bras has a good trick: he freezes fresh foie gras first, so it doesn't overcook on the outside and render away too much fat. To do this, cut the foie gras in slices and freeze, interleaved with freezer paper. If you like, serve the foie gras on thinly sliced fresh peach. **SERVES 6 AS A LIGHT DISH OR FIRST COURSE**

½ cup balsamic vinegar
1 fresh duck foie gras, about 1 pound
Sea salt and freshly ground black pepper

To serve
Peach Chutney (page 213)
Slices of hot brioche toast

1 Boil the balsamic vinegar to reduce it by half, then set aside to cool while you prepare the foie gras.

2 Fresh foie gras is easily damaged, so handle it with care. Let it soften for 20 minutes at room temperature so you can prise it apart gently without it breaking. There are two unequal halves connected by a thick blood vessel that runs across both sides. Using a table knife, work your way through the soft rich flesh, carefully pulling the tube away. You may find it useful to have a thin pair of scissors handy to snip into awkward areas. Don't worry too much if you break bits off accidentally, as you can reshape these inside the lobe, but try to keep it as intact as possible. Also don't worry about smaller veins – these dissolve on cooking. Cut the foie gras into six slices.

3 Heat a non-stick frying pan and, when you can feel a good heat rising, add the slices of foie gras – no need for any oil, as there is enough fat in the livers already. Season during cooking. Cook for about a minute on each side. Do not overcook – the slices will carry on cooking a little while they are resting out of the pan. The outside should be deliciously caramelized and the insides still pink and creamy.

4 Serve with the pan juices poured over and the balsamic vinegar trickled around. Accompany with peach chutney and brioche toast.

Loin of Beef with Watercress Purée

A top loin or strip roast comes from the short loin. It is a nice round shape, cooks well, and – more important – has a great flavor and texture. We buy it in 4½-pound roasts and "set" the shape by rolling it tightly into a ballotine and storing it in the fridge for 2 days. It can then be cut into thick steaks and broiled or pan-fried. We serve strip loin steaks with an eye-catching watercress purée that is embarrassingly simple to make. (In the restaurant we wring out the watercress purée in a cloth and serve it as a soft quenelle, but if you prefer a pouring sauce then use the maximum amount of cream.) Sit the steaks on a bed of sautéed mushrooms of your choice. I prefer chanterelles, but you can use cèpes, oyster mushrooms, or cremini.

SERVES 4 AS A MAIN DISH

1¼-pound piece beef top loin

3 tablespoons olive oil

1 tablespoon butter

7 ounces mushrooms (see above), sliced if large

2 fat cloves garlic, minced

2 teaspoons chopped fresh parsley

Sea salt and freshly ground black pepper

Sauce

10 ounces watercress leaves
   (about 3 cups)

4 ounces spinach leaves
   (about 1 cup)

¼–1 cup heavy cream

1 First, make the sauce. Put a pan of salted water on to boil. Push in all the watercress and boil for 5 minutes. Add the spinach and cook for another minute or so until wilted. Drain in a colander. Press with the back of a ladle to extract as much moisture as possible.

2 Put the leaves into a food processor and blend to a fine purée, scraping down the sides occasionally. Pour ¼ cup of the cream through the processor funnel and keep the blades whirling for what seems like an eternity. You will eventually get a sauce with a texture like silk. It will be so smooth, you will not need to pass it through a sieve. If you want a pouring sauce, add the remaining cream. Check the seasoning, and pour into a small saucepan ready for reheating.

3 Cut the beef loin into 4 even steaks and rub each side using 1 tablespoon oil. Heat a heavy, non-stick frying pan until you can feel a good heat rising. Lay in your steaks – they should give a good hiss as they hit the hot pan. Season the tops and cook for about 3 minutes, then flip over and cook the other side for 2 minutes. Slip the butter into the pan at this stage and season the second side. Remove the steaks from the pan and leave to rest while you cook the mushrooms.

4 Sauté the mushrooms with the garlic in the remaining oil. Season and mix with the parsley.

5 Reheat the watercress purée/sauce. Place the steaks on warmed plates (sliced first if you like), trickle any pan juices over, and spoon on the mushrooms. If your watercress purée is firm, shape it into quenelles. If it is a sauce, spoon some over the steaks and pass the rest separately. Serve with whatever accompaniment you like to eat steak with. Fries are great (see my recipe on page 197), or why not try slices of really fresh baguette?

Cherry Soup with Caramel-Balsamic Ice Cream

In July, 1998, I was privileged to cook for the World Cup Final dinner held in the Orangery in Versailles. What a night! The planning required several trips to Paris, and on one of these I visited a restaurant where I was served a fruit soup with the most amazing ice cream. It turned out to be a caramel flavor to which had been added aged balsamic vinegar. For the soup, you need deep red cherries to give not only flavor but also a rich mahogany color. **SERVES 4**

2¹/₂ cups dark red cherries, pitted
Scant 1 cup Stock Syrup (page 214)
3–4 leaves fresh lemon balm

Ice cream
1¹/₄ cups sugar
3 tablespoons balsamic vinegar
6 egg yolks
2 cups milk
²/₃ cup heavy cream

1 First, make the caramel for the ice cream. Put the sugar into a heavy-based saucepan and slowly heat until it starts to melt. (You might want to add a couple of tablespoons of water to help the process, and you can stir gently once or twice. True chefs, however, make caramel without water!) If you get crystals around the edge of the pan, wash them down with a pastry brush dipped in water. Stir occasionally until the crystals have all dissolved. When all the sugar has melted, slowly raise the heat and boil the sugar syrup until it starts to turn golden brown and then a mid-brown. Have ready a big bowl of ice water. As soon as the syrup is the right color, immerse the base of the pan in the water to cool the caramel. When cool, stir in the balsamic vinegar and set aside.

2 Now make the custard for the ice cream. Place the egg yolks in a bowl set on a damp cloth (which holds it steady) and whisk until pale golden. Bring the milk and cream slowly to a boil in a heavy-based saucepan. Slowly pour the creamy milk onto the yolks, whisking steadily. When it is all incorporated, tip back into the saucepan and return to a low heat. Stir until the mixture just starts to thicken (it should be 160–170°). Do not allow it even to start to bubble, or it may curdle. Remove and cool.

3 Make the soup: Reserve half the cherries (I'd suggest the best looking ones), and cut them in half if large. Roughly chop the rest. Bring the stock syrup to a boil and add the chopped cherries and lemon balm leaves. Remove from the heat and leave to infuse for about 15 minutes, then remove the lemon balm.

4 Blend the fruit and syrup mixture in a food processor or blender until smooth, then pass through a sieve into a bowl, rubbing through with the back of a ladle. Chill the soup.

5 Back to the ice cream. Mix the cooled caramel into the cool custard. Pour into an ice cream machine and churn until icy, smooth, and creamy. Scoop into a rigid plastic food container and freeze until just solid.

6 When ready to serve, divide the soup among four chilled shallow bowls. Sit a scoop of ice cream in the center and drop the reserved cherries around the ice cream. Serve immediately.

Wild Strawberry Shortbreads

As a Scot, I'm partial to a nice crisp shortbread, but I prefer to make mine using a pâte sablée *dough. I cut out elegant cookies the size of a coffee saucer and press a slight dip in the center. After baking, this is filled with a thick strawberry coulis, and dainty wild strawberries (fraises des bois) are arranged around the edge. Wild strawberries, originally from mountainous regions of Europe (hence the alternative name Alpine), are a different species from the common ones – their seeds stick up, while cultivated fruits have seeds that press into the flesh.* SERVES 6

8 ounces ripe strawberries, hulled

1 tablespoon sugar, or to taste

A squeeze of lemon juice

2 tablespoons thick heavy cream

About 10 ounces wild strawberries, hulled

Shortbreads

6 extra large egg yolks

$\frac{1}{2}$ cup + 2 tablespoons sugar,
  plus extra for sprinkling

$\frac{1}{2}$ cup (1 stick) unsalted butter, softened

$1\frac{1}{4}$ cups all-purpose flour, plus extra
  for rolling

$1\frac{1}{2}$ teaspoons baking powder

1 First, make the shortbread dough. Beat the egg yolks with the sugar until thick and creamy, then gradually beat in the butter. Sift the flour and baking powder together, and mix in. Knead lightly to a soft dough, then wrap in plastic wrap and chill for 30 minutes.

2 On a lightly floured board, roll out the dough to a $\frac{1}{4}$-inch thickness. Cut out 6 disks about 5 inches diameter, re-rolling as necessary. Use a coffee saucer as a template. Place on a non-stick baking sheet, and prick the disks a few times with a fork. Press the centers to make a slight dip and, if you like, pinch the edges into a slight rim. Chill for 30 minutes.

3 Preheat the oven to 300°. Sprinkle the disks with a little sugar and bake for 12 minutes or until pale golden. Allow to sit on the baking sheet for a minute to firm, then, using a metal spatula to help, slide onto a wire rack to cool and crisp.

4 Process the large strawberries to a purée, adding sugar to taste plus a squeeze of lemon juice and the heavy cream.

5 Just before serving, spoon the strawberry coulis into the center of the shortbreads, and arrange wild strawberries around the edge. Serve with sweetened, lightly whipped cream.

Pannacotta with Raspberries

One of my very favorite restaurants, I'm delighted to say, is in Scotland. It's Le Potinière at Gullane near Edinburgh, run by Hilary and David Brown. Hilary's food is perfect simplicity, the best in flavor, seasonality, and presentation. It's what the Scots do best, every mouthful memorable. This is her recipe for pannacotta, with a caramel base, simple and sublime. Needless to say, Scottish raspberries are a blissful match. Otherwise, out of season, try slices of ripe star fruit soaked in a grenadine-flavored syrup. **SERVES 6–8**

1³/₄ cups sugar
¹/₄ cup light corn syrup
2¹/₂ cups heavy cream
²/₃ cup milk
3 leaves gelatin
2 tablespoons rum
About 3 cups fresh raspberries

1 First, make the caramel. Put 1 cup of the sugar into a heavy-based saucepan with the corn syrup (this keeps the caramel viscous when cool) and ¹/₄ cup water. Place over a low heat and stir occasionally until the liquid no longer feels gritty. Make sure there are no sugar grains clinging to the sides of the pan either. Meanwhile, fill a bowl with ice water.

2 Raise the heat and allow the syrup to bubble until it reaches a nice caramel color, 345° on a candy thermometer. Do not stir the syrup at all while it is bubbling. As soon as the caramel is ready, remove it from the heat and lower the base of the pan carefully into the ice water. Hold the pan there for a minute or two until the temperature drops. This stops the syrup from continuing to cook and burning. Remove from the water and set aside to cool a bit.

3 Now make the cream. Put the cream and milk into a large saucepan and bring slowly to a boil. When the liquid starts to creep up the sides of the pan, adjust the heat so it maintains a medium boil, and hold it at this for about 5 minutes so the liquid reduces down a little.

4 Meanwhile, put the gelatin leaves into a bowl of cold water to soak for a few minutes until they soften, then drain off all the water.

5 Stir the remaining sugar and the rum into the boiling cream and allow to dissolve. Remove from the heat and cool for a few seconds, then slip in the softened gelatin and stir well until dissolved. Set aside to cool.

6 Place 6–8 dariole molds or other small cylindrical molds of ¹/₂-cup capacity on a tray. Spoon about 2 teaspoons of the warm caramel into each. Slowly pour in the cream, right up to the top. Chill until set.

7 To serve, dip the dariole molds in hot water for a few seconds, then pull the set cream away from the sides of the mold. Invert and shake out onto individual dessert plates. (Wet these first with cold water, so you can slide the pannacotta into position should it come out offside, then wipe the moisture off with a paper towel.) Arrange raspberries around each pannacotta and trickle any leftover caramel over.

Fruit Salad in a Glass

For this you need a glorious selection of fresh fruits from the summer harvest. Lemon balm, or balm, grows well in town and country gardens, or you can buy sprigs from specialty markets. Alternatively, use fresh mint with a touch of fresh lemon zest. Serve in tall elegant glasses with a spoonful of shaved Champagne sherbet on top. Champagne is the wine I use for this refreshing ice, but any good, dry sparkling white wine would do. Or try it with pink Champagne. The texture is light and crunchy, like an Italian granita. **SERVES 4**

2 Granny Smith apples

2 ripe Comice pears

1 ripe yellow peach

1 large orange

$^1/_2$ cup Stock Syrup (page 214)

Juice of 1 small lemon

1 large star fruit

5 sprigs fresh lemon balm

8 ounces mixed fresh summer berries
   (such as strawberries, raspberries,
   and red or white currants)

Champagne sherbet

$1^1/_4$ cups sugar

3 tablespoons light corn syrup

$1^1/_2$ cups Champagne

To decorate (optional)

Sugared cilantro leaf
   (page 205)

1 First, make the sherbet. Dissolve the sugar in $^3/_4$ cup water over a gentle heat, stirring occasionally. Add the corn syrup. Simmer for 5 minutes, then pour in the Champagne and remove at once from the heat. Allow to cool, then pour into a shallow freezerproof container and chill. When cold, freeze until partially frozen.

2 Remove and whisk with a strong metal fork so the crystals are broken up to a slush. Re-freeze lightly again, then repeat the whisking to make a gritty texture. Seal the container and store in the freezer until required. (This makes about 3 cups of sherbet.)

3 Core the apples and pears, then slice thinly (no need to peel). Peel, pit, and slice the peach. Peel and section the orange. Toss the prepared fruit with the stock syrup and lemon juice in a bowl. Slice the star fruit and mix into the bowl along with the lemon balm. Leave to infuse for about 15 minutes, then discard the lemon balm.

4 About 10 minutes before serving, remove the sherbet from the freezer and let it soften at room temperature.

5 Hull the strawberries and cut in half. Remove the stems from the currants, if using. Mix the berries gently into the fruit salad.

6 Spoon the fruit salad into four tall wine glasses, and top with any leftover syrup. Scrape the sherbet out of the freezer container with a metal spoon so you obtain slushy shavings, like snow, and spoon them on top of each glass. Serve immediately.

Mille-Feuille of Chocolate with Lavender

Lavender is an herb we normally associate with bathing, not baking. But in the parts of Europe where it grows in profusion (Provence in France, in particular), it is often sprinkled into bread doughs and sweet baking. I steep a spoonful of dried lavender heads in a light chocolate ganache, which I pipe between thin, crisp puff pastry wafers. I continue the floral fragrance by serving this with scoops of lavender ice cream (follow the recipe for Thyme Ice Cream on page 214, substituting 2 teaspoons of dried lavender flowers for the sprigs of thyme). **SERVES 4**

About 10 ounces puff pastry, preferably homemade (page 214)
1 cup Crème Anglaise (page 214)
2 teaspoons dried lavender flowers
10 ounces bittersweet chocolate (we use Valrhona),
  broken in small chunks
1 cup heavy cream
Unsweetened cocoa powder for dusting

1 Roll out the pastry to a rectangle slightly larger than 12 by 16 inches, which will allow enough excess so you can trim the edges neatly. (It is important to get even shapes for serving.)
Cut into four long rectangles of 4 by 12 inches. Using a long metal spatula, lift these onto a baking sheet and score each across into four equal rectangles. Chill for 20 minutes while you preheat the oven to 400°.
2 Bake for 10 minutes, then place another heavy baking sheet on top of the pastry rectangles (this helps to keep them flat). Bake for another 10–12 minutes until golden brown and crisp. Remove and cool on a wire rack.
3 Now for the cream. Warm the crème anglaise gently and stir in the lavender flowers. Leave to steep off the heat for 30 minutes, then strain and discard the flowers.
4 Return the crème anglaise to a gentle heat to warm again, then remove and stir in the chocolate. Leave until melted, then whisk until shiny. Set aside to cool.
5 Whip the heavy cream until it is softly stiff. Fold into the chocolate mixture.
6 Make four layered "sandwiches" with the pastry rectangles and chocolate cream, either spreading or piping the cream in between the pastry layers. Dust the tops with cocoa powder. Serve with small scoops or quenelles of lavender or vanilla ice cream.

Jasmine Custards

If you are looking for a variation on the crème brûlée theme, try this. Jasmine is in flower anytime from midsummer through to early fall. I've seen jasmine in flower in June and in early October, hanging over various town gardens around my part of London. You'll need a large mugful of the delicate white flowers for this recipe. Incidentally, if you are given a potted jasmine plant as a present for indoors, when it has finished flowering, plant it against a sunny wall or fence in the garden. Within a year or two you'll have a good supply of flowers. **SERVES 6**

1½ cups heavy cream
1 cup whole milk
2 ounces fresh jasmine flowers
6 extra large egg yolks
6 tablespoons granulated sugar
Demerara or other coarse brown sugar for caramelizing (optional)

1 Heat the cream and milk in a saucepan and allow the liquid to rise up the sides of the pan before removing from the heat. Stir in the jasmine flowers and leave until cold.

2 Strain into a clean heavy-based pan, pressing the flowers in the sieve with the back of a ladle to extract the fragrance.

3 Preheat the oven to 275°. Reheat the cream. Meanwhile, beat the egg yolks in a large bowl, set on a damp cloth to keep it steady. When the cream starts to creep up the sides of the pan again, pour a small amount onto the yolks and whisk to blend. Keep whisking in the hot liquid, in cautious amounts so it doesn't curdle.

4 Strain the mixture back into the pan and stir in the granulated sugar. Heat on the lowest possible setting, stirring frequently, until the custard coats the back of the spoon. Pour into six elegant heatproof containers such as ramekins or pretty heatproof teacups.

5 Bake the custards for 45–60 minutes until the sides come away from the edge of the container when tipped slightly. The center should remain slightly wobbly. Remove and cool, then chill until set.

6 If you like, you can sprinkle some Demerara sugar on top and caramelize this with a blowtorch before serving.

fall

I don't enjoy too much summer heat. In fact, when the days begin to shorten and we wake to an autumnal nip in the air, I do feel a tinge of relief. And excitement too, because with the fall comes the promise of bountiful harvests of fruits and vegetables at their best.

Of all the leafy vegetables that pass through my kitchen, I suppose **sorrel** is one of the most tricky to handle. The peppery, astringent taste is terrific in lifting the flavor of fish dishes (especially poached salmon), soups, and salads, but knowing when to add it is the key to success. If added too soon, the leaves wilt to a slimy, dull green, so it is best to put it in at the last minute. Cooks sometimes add a handful of baby spinach leaves to a sorrel dish to enhance the color, but I find this unnecessary if you leave it until the last moment. If you grow sorrel, pick the leaves just before you need them. The ideal size for flavor is about the length of a large bay leaf. Peel the fine fibers from the stem, then shred the leaves. They are delicate and bruise easily, even more so than basil, so always use the sharpest knife you can.

I'm really fortunate in having had a number of proud moments in my career. One of the highlights of the summer of 1999, was cooking a celebration lunch for the opening of the Scottish Parliament at Kincardine House. But there was another memorable event that day. It was my first taste of spanking fresh **spinach** picked barely a few minutes before and brought into the kitchen by the gardener himself. Where would we be now without spinach in the kitchen? Modern market gardening and transport have made this wonderful vegetable indispensable. But like sorrel, it must not be overcooked and is best added at the last minute. In the fall, spinach leaves are larger but still wonderfully tender, and they can be used for soups and for serving under medallions of fish or pink meat. Blanch the leaves for a few seconds in boiling water, then immediately drain and refresh in a bowl of ice water. Press out the excess water, then reheat at the last minute with a bit of butter.

The last few years have seen the popularizing of many vegetables that can now be easily grown under cover, including many exotics. One of the nicest is the ragged-leaf **wild arugula**, which to the untrained eye looks like a weed. More peppery and textured than the smoother, dark green arugula, wild arugula has a lot more uses than being tossed in a salad or used as a rustic garnish. The flavor is brilliant with full-flavored cheeses such as Parmesan and tangy goat cheese. Mixed with fresh goat cheese and vinaigrette it makes a wonderful filling for homemade ravioli. I also like it roughly chopped and tossed into risottos at the last moment.

No offense, but **celeriac** must be the ugliest vegetable around. Maybe that's why it is so underrated. I suppose it could be described as the Cyrano de Bergerac of the kitchen – ugly on the outside, but wonderful within. It's delicious as a purée, brilliant in soups, good deep-fried as vegetable "fries," or grated raw as a salad, and perfect cooked fondant-style (sautéed first and then simmered in stock). In the fall I like a truly decadent treat of creamed celeriac topped with shavings of Périgord truffle. Sometimes as an *amuse-gueule*, we serve a tiny salad of shaved apple and celeriac bound in truffle vinaigrette. Celeriac is so versatile a vegetable, I really do enjoy cooking with it.

Looking a lot like chubby grubs, **crosnes** (see photograph on page 112) look and taste like a cross between globe artichokes and salsify, although they are completely unrelated. They were imported to France from China in the nineteenth century and grown in a village called Crosnes, from which they took their name (they're also called Chinese or Japanese artichokes). We treat them in a similar way to Jerusalem artichokes – cooked and then tossed in brown butter with chopped parsley and lemon juice. They're terrific with squab and also with full-flavored fish.

A truly versatile vegetable, **cauliflower** is good whatever way you want to use it. It does, however, have a downside, which is the smell if you overcook it even by a few minutes. I think that is what puts some people off eating it. My hint to lessen the smell (apart from watch the clock) is to simmer the florets in a mixture of water and milk. In the restaurant, we use only the actual florets, without any stem, although at home you might like to trim them longer.

Cauliflower is tremendous with fish, especially sweet scallops. We have one recipe where baby-size florets are dipped in a *beignet* batter and fried as fritters. We also slice large florets thinly, season

them with curry spices, salt, and pepper, and then fry them in olive oil until they are beautifully caramelized. When cooled to room temperature, we serve the slices with a simple dressing of puréed raisins, capers, and water.

Another vegetable we put on for our fall menus is **fennel**. I prefer to use baby fennel – the little hearts look like crab claws and, appropriately, are brilliant served with all kinds of fish dishes. I like the baby vegetables because they are very tender, yet still possess a full aniseed flavor. Older fennel bulbs need to be peeled of the stringy outside fibers. Fennel is a popular Mediterranean vegetable, especially in the South of France. In Tunisia and Morocco, you see carts piled high with crisp fennel bulbs, to be served no doubt alongside spicy lamb dishes and chargrilled chicken and fish. We like to top and tail baby fennel bulbs, then cook them whole in olive oil until lightly colored.

The **eggplant** holds a special place in my heart. A few days before opening my first restaurant in Park Walk, London, we still hadn't thought of a name for it, or rather agreed on one. In a flash it came to me – the Aubergine, which is the French name for eggplant. You can stuff eggplants, cube and stew them, even fry thinly as "chips," and use in almost anything from canapés to main courses. And this vegetable can get a cook out of trouble when faced with having to prepare a hearty dish for non-meat eaters. The only thing you cannot do is eat eggplants raw. If you intend roasting, stewing, or grilling them, they do not need to be salted first (we call this dégorging), but if you want to fry them, it is best to draw out excess moisture first. Sprinkle lightly with fine sea salt and drain in a colander for 20 minutes. Then rinse well and pat dry.

Eggplants can absorb a lot of oil, if you let them. To avoid this, I toss them first in oil, then brown them in a smoking hot, dry pan. To make a creamy purée, we halve the eggplants, slash the flesh a few times, brush both sides with olive oil, season, and put back together with slivers of garlic and sprigs of fresh rosemary inside. Wrapped in foil and baked in a hot oven, they take about 40 minutes for the flesh to soften enough to scoop out and purée. But we haven't finished yet. The purée is heated in a dry frying pan until reduced down a little, to drive off excess moisture, then it is mixed with minced tomatoes, fresh cilantro, extra virgin olive oil, and seasoning, to make a sublime eggplant "caviar" – the basis for many of my early hallmark dishes.

One of my most fraught moments during the preparation of the World Cup Dinner for over 700 people in July, 1998, at Versailles in Paris, was the preparation of a garnish of deep-fried zucchini leaves. These had to be dipped in a light batter, fried, and then pressed between two sheets of paper to flatten. I'm happy to say that we did manage to produce delicate, gossamer-thin leaves that looked fantastic. And this does nicely illustrate how versatile the zucchini is as a food plant. In the early fall it is at its best, and you can use the flowers, leaves, and, of course, the gourd itself as a vegetable. Zucchini contain a lot of water, so suit light cooking. We never boil them, preferring to slice them thinly and then sauté in a little olive oil, or souse in a vinaigrette. And, of course, they're a classic partner for eggplant in ratatouille. Try this idea for an appetizer, following the recipe for Tomato and Parmesan Gratinée Tarts on page 133, substituting zucchini for the tomatoes. After baking the pastry bases, spread with a little tapenade and arrange thinly sliced, sautéed zucchini over this. Top each tart with a thin slice of seared fresh tuna.

Perhaps because the U.K. is an island (and proud of it), we sometimes close our minds to foods that we think of as a bit "foreign." One of these is pumpkin – for a long time we have only associated it with Halloween. Our markets have pumpkins in stock for about two weeks at the end of October, and then bang, they disappear almost overnight. What do people do with all that lovely flesh they've scraped out when making the jack o'lanterns, I wonder? Slowly, we are realizing just how versatile pumpkin is, and the fact that there are several varieties. In the restaurant we like to use the pale green pumpkin with ridges, popular in France and with West Indian cooks. You don't have to buy a whole one, just a wedge or two will do nicely. And far from being in season just for a few weeks, you'll find pumpkins on sale in markets during the fall and well into the winter. We make a smooth golden soup with pumpkin, served with spicy fried scallops, and also use it as a ravioli filling. To thicken the flesh for the filling, after cooking we put it in a jelly bag and leave to drain overnight. Pumpkin makes a good simple purée to serve with rich meats such as venison or game, and "marries" well with smoky pancetta and punchy Parmesan cheese. It has its sweet uses too. I love pumpkin with the Italian mostarda di fruta, and in a pumpkin and frangipane tart, which I ate when I was a young chef in Paris.

No piece on autumn foods could appear without a good discourse on wild mushrooms. We always look forward to the boxes of fascinating fungi our suppliers bring in at this time of year. One of my special favorites is the tiny mousseron from France, which is also called the St. George mushroom. It may look dainty, but packs a lot of flavor. We use mousserons in soups, especially with mussels, and also serve them along with globe artichokes as a garnish vegetable for veal and squab. Another favorite is cèpes – sometimes as much as 25 pounds a day of cèpes will pass through the kitchen, to be sautéed, confit, roasted, or packed in jars with olive oil. We even hang them to dry until brittle, then grind them to a fine powder, to scatter over risottos and fillets of sea bass. Possibly the ugliest of the wild mushrooms, black trumpets look dark and sinister. I love to serve them in warm salads or with roasted fillets of turbot. Occasionally, when we can get them, we put blewits on the menu. Their flesh is quite bitter, so we counter this by making sure they are well and truly sautéed, even to the point of overcooking. Then we stir in a spoonful of confit of sweet shallots to temper the flavor.

I associate mussels with my first serious telling-off as a young chef in Paris. You see, in French restaurants, the hygiene regulations regarding mussels are very strict, and each chef who opens up a sack must pin the identifying tag to a board. Then, in the unlikely event of food poisoning, the source of supply can be traced back. As the young "rosbif" from England, I knew nothing of this and threw out the tag. Fortunately, I wasn't fluent in French then (I am now), so didn't quite

a time into the water. Then, after peeling, we stack them in tight rows on trays and chill to firm the flesh. Their heads are full of flavor, so we sauté them to use in a langoustine stock for sauces. The heads also contain a membrane that acts as a clarifying agent for stocks, just like the albumen in egg whites – after simmering, we find the liquid has become naturally clear. Langoustines are popular as ravioli fillings, or sautéed to serve with salads or in soups. We often dust them with curry powder or crushed saffron before roasting, and, for a really strong color, sometimes dip them into green lobster coral, which cooks to a vibrant pink.

Throughout the summer and fall months, we feature **red mullet** frequently on the menu. It is obligingly good both hot and cold. Most of my red mullet ideas come from my time in the Mediterranean – like serving crisp-skinned fillets topped with a fine black olive purée (we call this a tapenade, although I omit the usual anchovies, as they are too overpowering), or placing them on couscous scented with lemongrass. And, of course, red mullet is one of the essential fish for a classic bouillabaisse. This we serve with croûtes topped with the chopped and sautéed mullet liver mixed with olive purée. We also simply pan-fry red mullet fillets or souse them in a vinaigrette.

The skin of red mullet is the great attraction for me, so delicate and pretty. The scales can be easily picked off with fingers (we do this inside large plastic garbage bags). To get a firmer grip when filleting, my chefs bend the fish in a slight curve before cutting down the backbone. It's a neat trick. The bones and heads make good fish stock.

understand the "finer points" of the abuse hurled at me by chef. Ouch! Two better memories of mussels in France are baking them in the shell with brioche crumbs and Gruyère cheese, and the delightful style of matching mussels with mushrooms, which the French call *terre et mer* (earth and sea).

Hardly a day goes by when we don't have **langoustines**, also called Dublin Bay prawns, on the menu. They are indispensable as a fine food and have so many uses. Our langoustines come to us from the west of Scotland. They are transported in aerated tanks, which makes them very frisky by the time we receive them. If you flick their tails, they snap straight back, certainly a sign of being very much alive. We find they peel easier if blanched for 25 seconds in boiling water, dropping just a dozen at

Once derided as tasteless and watery, **monkfish** now occupies a supreme place in fish cuisine and it is in danger of culinary overkill. Like cod, we are in danger of overfishing it. You see, monkfish is a deep water fish and so is difficult to farm. It takes many years for monkfish to grow to maturity, so replenishment of stocks is slow, and supply is now falling behind demand. It is the tails we eat – the heavy, bony heads are discarded. (The livers are tasty and can be cooked to serve as a garnish.) There is only one central bone, or cartilage, with two fillets on each side. These have to be skinned and the gray membrane carefully removed because it can cause the flesh to curl unattractively during cooking. After filleting, we often roll the flesh tightly in plastic wrap, to tighten and firm it. For a few months I was Pierre Koffman's head chef at Tante Claire in London (now the site of my restaurant), and I remember well a brilliant monkfish recipe he did – a fillet tunneled out and stuffed with a finely minced ratatouille, then wrapped in a whole flattened, scored squid to be pan-roasted. Sheer genius. He served that with a saffron-scented risotto.

Unlike monkfish, **rabbit** is not in short supply. The French and Italians have a particular fondness for it and cook it like chicken or lean tender pork, with fresh rosemary or thyme. And hip New Yorkers are taking to it in their chic upscale eateries. We Brits still associate rabbit with flopsy bunny (or field vermin), although it is beginning to feature on some restaurant menus. We use the shoulder meat for stews (*pot au feu*), terrines, and pâtés, and roast the saddles and legs. The carcasses make good stock, which can then be used to make a setting-strength aspic jelly for pâtés *en gelée*. The legs and shoulders we also *confit* slowly in goose fat until the tender meat can be pulled into shreds, then mix it with vinaigrette. Rabbit is good with gnocchi and a light and creamy mustard sauce, and with a caramelized tart of Belgian endive. And the tiny rib chops can be served with the kidneys as a garnish.

Fall is the time for game birds. The shooting seasons in the U.K. start in late summer, although some, such as squab, are on sale year round. I had my first hunting experience with Marco Pierre White. His aim was much surer than mine – not only did he bag his birds in flight, but also the ones I missed. But I'll learn… We get **squab** (wood pigeons) in from Anjou in France, where they are reared in the wild. Most of the time we use only the breasts of wild birds, although the legs can be carved off too. The carcasses make good stock. The breasts are nice served sliced in a warm salad, and we use them as part of a game terrine such as the Mosaic of Autumn Game on page 130. Squabs are particularly delicious served with a soft rutabaga purée and the little artichoke-flavored crosnes. We often pan-fry **pheasant** breasts with fresh thyme or serve with a salad of apple and celeriac tossed with a walnut vinaigrette. Older birds are used in a fricassee with lentils. If the birds have been badly shot, we use the meat to make a sausage bound with foie gras. Little dark-fleshed **wild ducks** taste like a cross between woodcock and grouse, and a lot gamier than normal ducks. Their legs are tough and sinewy, so we use a part poaching, part grilling method of cooking. Because the breasts are lean, we cook them on the bone and serve them pink.

Perhaps the foods we associate most with autumn are apples and pears. We like Cox's Orange Pippin **apples** for *tarte Tatin* – Cox's make good tart fillings because they contain less water than many other apple varieties. Their flavor is also brilliant in parfaits because it is so distinctive. We dry wafer-thin apple slices as *tuiles*, to use as a pretty decoration. Sometimes in the fall we mix lightly poached apples with chopped prunes and serve topped with an apple gratinée.

The flavor of **pears** is beautifully rounded and needs little else in the way of flavoring. Comice, Bartlett, and Bosc pears are all ideal for cooking, as long as they are slightly underripe and firm – too soft and they taste floury and have lost their edge of flavor. There are savory uses for pears, such as in a fruit relish for foie gras (flavored with a hint of saffron). For desserts, pears are great for poaching in a spiced red wine syrup to be served with a rich peppercorn-flavored crème anglaise and, like apples, they make a good compote. Their flowery fragrance is also nicely complemented by a hint of lime. We also dry thin slices of pear, then sandwich them together with a cinnamon ice cream, standing them upright on a compote of pears in red wine.

Lentil and Langoustine Soup

I do enjoy classic rustic dishes, especially those served with an elegant twist. This recipe is a lentil velouté served very thick and smooth and topped with roasted langoustines that float proud of the rich liquid underneath. I use the recipe as a "teaser" to whet diners' appetites in my restaurant, but double or even triple the quantity will make a normal-size first course portion. **SERVES 4–6 AS A FIRST COURSE**

1¼ cups *lentilles de Puy*

1 medium carrot, chopped in two or three

1 onion, quartered

1 fat clove garlic, peeled and left whole

1 fresh bouquet garni (bay leaf, sprig
   fresh thyme, some parsley stems,
   and celery leaves tied together)

4 cups Dark Chicken Stock (page 212)
   or Vegetable *Nage* (page 212)

A couple of drops of truffle oil

²/₃ cup heavy cream

8–12 raw langoustines (or jumbo shrimp),
   peeled

A few large pinches of curry powder

2 tablespoons olive oil

Sea salt and freshly ground black pepper

1 Place the lentils (no need to soak) in a large saucepan with the vegetables, garlic, and bouquet garni. Cover well with cold water and bring to a boil. Cook on a medium heat until the lentils just start to "explode." This should take about 15 minutes – no longer or they will turn mushy.

2 Drain the lentils, reserving about 1 cup of the cooking liquid. Discard all the vegetables, garlic, and bouquet garni. Blend the softened lentils in a food processor or blender, adding the reserved liquid to make a silky-smooth purée.

3 Return to the pan and "let down" with the stock or *nage*. Season and bring to a boil, stirring. Add the truffle oil and cream. That's it!

4 To cook the langoustines, dust them with the curry powder and seasoning. Heat a non-stick pan and, when you can feel a good heat rising, add the oil. Stir-fry the langoustines for a minute or so on each side until they turn pink and just firm.

5 Reheat the soup and pour into six warmed soup bowls. Top each serving with two langoustines and serve.

Potage of Potato and Leek

This is just the sort of soup someone learning to cook should begin with. But although simple, it can be turned into the ultimate in sophistication simply by adding a few lightly poached oysters or topping with small spoonfuls of whipped cream and Osietra caviar.

SERVES 4 AS A FIRST COURSE

8 ounces leeks (pale green and white only), diced (about 2½ cups)

1 small onion, chopped

1 tablespoon olive oil

1 tablespoon butter

¼ cup dry white wine

1 large potato, peeled and diced (about 2 cups)

1 fresh bouquet garni (a few parsley stems, sprig fresh thyme, small bay leaf, and sprig of celery leaves tied together)

3 cups Light Chicken Stock (page 212) or Vegetable *Nage* (page 212)

½ cup light cream

Sea salt and freshly ground black pepper

1 Put the leeks and onion into a large saucepan with the oil and butter. When they start to sizzle, cover and sweat the vegetables over a low heat for 5 minutes.

2 Add the wine and cook uncovered until evaporated. Add the potato and bouquet garni, cover with the stock or *nage*, and bring to a boil. Season and simmer for 15 minutes until the potato is soft.

3 Remove the bouquet garni. You can leave this soup chunky, as the vegetables are chopped small, and the potato should by now have dissolved into the liquid, thickening it slightly. However, if you favor a silky texture, then purée either in a food processor or blender, or in the pan with an immersion blender.

4 Stir in the cream and season to taste. A good soup for any meal occasion.

Cauliflower and Sorrel Soup

A simple cream soup, this is ideal for when the nights start to draw in and you realize it's time to think about food for chilly weather. There are still leaves of spiky sorrel in the garden, and you don't need too many for this soup – just enough to lift the creamy color. For a touch of class, treat your guests to a caviar garnish. In the summer you can serve this soup lightly chilled.

SERVES 6 AS A FIRST COURSE

1 large head cauliflower, stem discarded,
   florets chopped

1 medium potato, peeled and chopped

½ onion, chopped

1 tablespoon butter

1 tablespoon olive oil

4 cups Light Chicken Stock (page 212)
   or Vegetable *Nage* (page 212)

2 cups whole milk

½ cup heavy cream

6 large sorrel leaves, stems trimmed,
   then shredded

2 tablespoons caviar (optional)

Sea salt and freshly ground black pepper

1 Place the cauliflower florets, potato, and onion in a saucepan with the butter and oil. Heat gently and, when the contents start to sizzle, cover with a lid and sweat everything over a low heat for about 10 minutes. The vegetables should not be at all colored.

2 Add the stock or *nage* and bring to a boil, then pour in the milk and return gently to a boil. (This way, there will be no scum forming from the milk.) Season to taste, then simmer, uncovered, for 10–15 minutes when the vegetables should be soft.

3 Pour in half the cream, then purée in a food processor or blender, or blend in the pan with an immersion blender. Pass the purée through a sieve into a clean pan, rubbing with the back of a ladle.

4 Stir in the rest of the cream. Taste for seasoning and bring the soup to a boil. Ladle into soup plates, top with the sorrel shreds, and add a spoonful of caviar to each. Serve.

Marinated Tuna Salad

Tuna is a dense, meaty fish so you need a smaller portion size than other fish, no more than 4 ounces. The flesh is also affected by the way it is caught – the tail end is less likely to have any signs of congealed blood. So try to buy a piece of loin from the tail end. After searing in hot oil, marinate the tuna in a coriander-flavored dressing. Then serve with soused autumn vegetables.

SERVES 6 AS A FIRST COURSE OR 4 AS A LIGHT DISH

1-pound loin of tuna, from the tail end

3 tablespoons olive oil

²/₃ cup Classic Vinaigrette (page 213)

1 teaspoon coriander seeds, lightly crushed

1 tablespoon chopped fresh cilantro

2 stalks salsify

A large squeeze of lemon juice

2 globe artichokes

4 ounces snow peas, chopped

1 small onion, sliced

2 medium carrots, thinly sliced

2 tablespoons aged balsamic vinegar

Sea salt and freshly ground black pepper

1 Slice the tuna loin into two long fillets. Heat 1 tablespoon of the oil in a heavy-based frying pan (or a ridged griddle pan if you want attractive chargrilled stripes on the tuna). Sear the fillets for 2 minutes all over – the flesh should still feel a little springy. Do not overcook tuna, or it will toughen and dry out. Transfer to a dish.

2 Mix half the vinaigrette with the coriander seeds, then pour over the tuna fillets. Press the fresh cilantro over the surface. Cover and leave to steep for 1 hour.

3 Meanwhile, peel the salsify and cut into sticks. Cook in boiling salted water with the lemon juice for 5 minutes. Remove with a slotted spoon, refresh, and set aside.

4 Cut off the artichoke stalks, pull off the leaves, and cut out the hairy choke to leave the meaty bottom. (See photographs of this technique on page 216.) Cut the bottom into pieces. Cook in the lemon water for 10 minutes. Drain.

5 Blanch the snow peas in boiling water for 1 minute, then drain and refresh under cold running water. Drain and pat dry.

6 Heat the remaining oil in a saucepan, add the onion, and cook for 3 minutes. Add the carrots, salsify, and artichokes, and cook for a further 2–3 minutes. Finally, toss in the blanched snow peas and cook for 1 minute. Season nicely and stir in the balsamic vinegar and then the rest of the vinaigrette. Set aside to cool.

7 To serve, remove the tuna from the marinade (no need to scrape off the herbs unless you wish to). Cut the fillets into medallions. Divide the soused vegetables among the plates and place the tuna medallions on top.

Warm Salad of Squab with Honey-Soused Vegetables

Here is another first course that makes good use of the best foods in season. Root vegetables make delicious salads if cooked briefly and then left to cool in a marinade. Game breasts cooked pink and sliced thinly complement it all nicely. **SERVES 4 AS A FIRST COURSE**

4 ounces celeriac

4 ounces kohlrabi

1 small bulb fennel

4 ounces pearl onions

2–3 tablespoons olive oil

4 ounces baby carrots, scraped

2 ounces tiny mushrooms, such as
  chanterelles, trimmed

1 tablespoon butter

8 boneless squab breasts,
  about 3 ounces each

Sea salt and freshly ground black pepper

Marinade

1 shallot, minced

1 tablespoon olive oil

1 sprig fresh thyme (lemon thyme, if possible)

1 tablespoon sherry vinegar

1 tablespoon clear flower-scented honey

½ cup peanut oil

¼ cup hazelnut oil

Juice of 1 lime

1 First, make the marinade. Gently sauté the shallot in the olive oil with the thyme for about 5 minutes until softened but not colored. Deglaze with the vinegar and cook for a few seconds. Add the honey, peanut and hazelnut oils, and the lime juice plus some seasoning. Keep warm.

2 Peel the **celeriac** and kohlrabi and cut into cubes or *bâtons*, varying the lengths and shapes to add interest. Keep the thicknesses even so the vegetables cook nicely. Peel the outside ribs of the fennel with a swivel peeler, then cut lengthwise into wedges. Blanch the onions in boiling water for 2 minutes, then drain and peel.

3 Heat 1–2 tablespoons of olive oil in a heavy-based frying pan and stir in all the vegetables. Cook gently for 5–7 minutes, stirring occasionally, until they just begin to soften, but without coloring them. Remove from the heat and pour over three-fourths of the marinade. Leave the vegetables to cool in this for at least 2 hours. Do not chill, as they should be served at room temperature.

4 Now for the squab. Heat another tablespoon of olive oil with the butter in a heavy-based frying pan. Season the breasts and cook, skin-side down, for about 3 minutes. Flip the breasts over and cook the other side for 2–3 minutes. They should feel lightly springy when pressed. Season again. Leave for 3 minutes or so while you serve the vegetables.

5 Drain the vegetables of their marinade (this can be re-used should you wish). Divide among four plates. Slice the squab breasts on the diagonal, or leave them whole, and sit on top of the vegetables. Trickle some of the remaining marinade over and serve hot.

Salad of Cèpes and Langoustines in Mustard Dressing

Langoustines (a.k.a. Dublin Bay prawns) are a favorite ingredient. I generally opt for the biggest ones because the flesh is plump and sweet and remains moist when pan-roasted. To make them easier to peel, blanch just for 1 minute in boiling water. Apart from this, the salad is quite straightforward to prepare, and the colors and flavors come together so well on the plate.

SERVES 4 AS A FIRST COURSE

12 large raw langoustines (or jumbo shrimp)

3 tablespoons olive oil

8 ounces large fresh cèpes, bases trimmed,
  then thickly sliced

²/₃ cup Classic Vinaigrette (page 213)

1 slightly rounded tablespoon Dijon mustard

5 ounces baby spinach leaves (about 1½ cups)

A few large pinches of mild curry powder

Sea salt and freshly ground black pepper

Celery leaves for garnish, deep fried if you like

1 Bring a large pan of salted water to a boil, then drop in the langoustines. Boil for a minute, then drain and cool. When you are able to handle them (they are easier to peel when warm), pull off the heads and crack the top of the shell with the back of a knife. Then simply push up from the tail end and out should pop perfectly peeled, pink shellfish. Set aside.

2 Heat 2 tablespoons of the oil in a frying pan and, when really hot, sauté the cèpes until they are nicely colored and softened. Season well. Remove and cool.

3 Mix the vinaigrette with the mustard. Toss the cèpes with a third of the dressing. Set aside. Season the spinach and toss with another third of the dressing. Place in the center of four plates. (In the restaurant, we arrange the spinach leaves in a flower shape inside a large biscuit cutter – not possible, I know, when you are on your own.)

4 Season the langoustines and dust with pinches of curry power. Heat the last of the oil in a frying pan and, when really hot, sauté the langoustines quickly for a minute or two on each side. Cut each one in half, if large.

5 Spoon the mustardy cèpes in the center of the spinach, then top with the langoustines. Finally, trickle the last of the dressing over, garnish with celery leaves, and serve quickly.

Salade Tiède of Mushrooms, Mussels, and Crosnes

This is a good example of a style of dish the French call "terre et mer" – mixing foods of land and sea. It is a warm salad of mussels and two unusual ingredients found only during the fall, mousseron *mushrooms and crosnes.* Mousserons *are tiny, perfectly formed mushrooms with caps the size of M 'n' Ms. Their fairy size gives a false impression, for they are tough little things and respond well to high frying. Crosnes, or Chinese artichokes, are an unusual vegetable, with a good earthy flavor. Both* mousserons *and crosnes need particular preparation.*

SERVES 4 AS A FIRST COURSE

4 ounces *mousseron* mushrooms
  (or other small wild mushrooms)
2 tablespoons butter
2 tablespoons olive oil
10 ounces fresh mussels
1 bay leaf
1 sprig fresh thyme

½ cup dry white wine
4 ounces crosnes (or use
  baby Jerusalem artichokes)
1 tablespoon chopped
  fresh chervil or parsley
2 tablespoons heavy cream
Sea salt and freshly ground black pepper

1 Prepare this dish in stages, then bring everything together just before serving. First, the *mousserons*. Pick off the stems so you just have the caps. Heat half the butter in a frying pan and sauté them for 2–3 minutes until softened.

2 Drain off the juice and save it in a small saucepan. Wipe out the frying pan, then heat the remaining butter with a teaspoon of the oil until nice and hot. Sauté the *mousserons* again to get them nice and browned. Drain, saving the juices again, and set aside.

3 Wash the mussels well and pull off any beards. Scrub off the barnacles, too, if possible. Discard any mussels that don't close when you tap them. Heat an empty saucepan until very hot and tip in the mussels, together with the bay leaf, thyme, and wine. Clamp on the lid and cook for about 4 minutes.

4 Uncover the pan and drain the liquid into the saucepan with the *mousseron* juices. Discard any mussels that haven't opened. Pick out the meat of those that have and cool, then chill for 30 minutes to firm the flesh.

5 To prepare the crosnes, trim the ends if necessary, then place in a bowl with a little cold water and rub them between your hands with sea salt. This helps to scrub them clean. Rinse well.

6 Heat the remaining oil in a pan and sauté the crosnes until nicely colored, about 3 minutes. Tip the mussels into the pan and stir-fry until reheated. Toss in the *mousserons* and reheat, then divide among four soup plates. Sprinkle with the chervil or parsley.

7 Add the cream to the saved juices and bubble down until reduced by half. Spoon over the salad – there will be just enough sauce to moisten everything – and serve.

Pumpkin and Pancetta Risotto

It is a poor autumn kitchen indeed that does not have a plump pumpkin available. There are so many ways to take advantage of its creamy, sweet golden flesh, from soups and stews through to pasta fillings and pies. A risotto with a lightly browned diced pumpkin brunoise, *some smoky, crisp pancetta, and tangy Parmesan makes a good light meal.* **SERVES 4 AS A FIRST COURSE OR 2 AS A MAIN DISH**

$^1/_3$ cup chopped pancetta

2–2$^1/_2$ cups Light Chicken Stock (page 212)

2 large shallots, chopped

1 pound pumpkin flesh, cut into $^1/_2$-inch cubes (about 4 cups)

3 tablespoons olive oil

Scant 1 cup risotto rice (Carnaroli, Arborio, or Vialone Nano)

$^1/_2$ cup dry white wine

2 tablespoons mascarpone

$^1/_4$ cup freshly grated Parmesan cheese

Sea salt and freshly ground black pepper

1 Heat a dry non-stick frying pan and, when hot, fry the pancetta until browned and crisp. Drain and set aside. Heat the stock to a gentle simmer in a saucepan.

2 In a large saucepan, gently sauté the shallots and pumpkin in the oil for about 5 minutes. Stir in the rice and cook for a further 2 minutes to toast the grains. Pour in the wine and cook until reduced right down.

3 Now pour in one-fourth of the stock and stir well. Cook gently until the liquid has been absorbed, then stir in another ladleful of stock. Continue cooking and stirring, gradually adding the stock, until the rice grains are just tender and the risotto is creamy. The whole process should take about 15 minutes.

4 About 2 minutes before the end of cooking, stir in the pancetta, mascarpone, and half the Parmesan. Check the seasoning, then serve in warmed bowls, sprinkled with the remaining Parmesan.

Mosaic of Autumn Game

An attractive chunky terrine is the ultimate prepare-ahead appetizer. We don't use gelatin to set the layers, but rely instead on the natural setting properties of ham hocks. You will need a nice selection of game birds and, maybe for a special treat, some foie gras.

When serving, we spread a touch of truffle oil on the top of each slice to give an inviting gloss. This terrine is best with toasted brioche, but crusty baguette would be fine. It is good, too, with an apple and celeriac salad such as that on page 121, or some mixed salad leaves dressed with a hazelnut vinaigrette. **MAKES A 2¼-POUND TERRINE TO SERVE 6–8 AS A FIRST COURSE**

2 ham hocks

1 carrot, roughly chopped

1 onion, roughly chopped

1 stalk celery, roughly chopped

1 leek, roughly chopped

1 fresh bouquet garni (a bay leaf,
   sprig fresh thyme, parsley stems,
   and celery leaves tied together)

1 sprig fresh thyme

Meats

4 squab breasts

2 pheasant breasts

2 partridge breasts

2 free-range chicken breasts

8 ounces venison tenderloin

3 tablespoons each Madeira,
   ruby Port, and Cognac

2–3 tablespoons olive oil

Sea salt and freshly ground black pepper

1 If necessary, soak the ham hocks overnight in plenty of cold water to remove excess salt. For the meats, trim the breasts to neat shapes, discarding any skin, bone, fat, or sinews. Toss them all with the venison and alcohol, and leave overnight to impart flavor and stain the flesh.

2 The next day, drain the hocks and place in a large pan with the roughly chopped vegetables and bouquet garni. Bring slowly to a boil, skimming off any scum that forms on top. Simmer for 1½–2 hours until the meat is very tender, skimming often.

3 Leave the hocks to cool in the stock, then remove. Discard all skin and fat and pull the meat into thick shreds; set aside. Strain the stock, then bring to a boil and simmer with the fresh thyme sprig for about 10 minutes. Cool. Put some stock in a bowl and chill to test its setting strength. It should be firm. If not, boil the stock to reduce further, and check for setting again. When it will set firm, measure out 2 cups.

4 Drain the meats and pat dry. Heat the oil in a heavy-based frying pan and cook each meat separately: the chicken breasts for 4–5 minutes each side and the other meats for 3–4 minutes per side, depending on thickness. Cool on paper towels, adding seasoning as they cool.

5 Now assemble the terrine. Pour a little of the stock over the bottom of a 2½-pound (10-cup) terrine mold and allow to set in the refrigerator. Make your layers starting with thin slices of foie gras, if using, or a thin one of shredded ham. Place the breasts, venison tenderloin, and more shredded ham lengthwise on this. Spoon some of the setting stock over each layer – just enough hold the meats in place. When you've finished, place the terrine in the refrigerator to set until firm, at least overnight. Do not weigh down.

6 To serve, dip the terrine briefly in a bowl of scalding hot water to the count of 5 to unmold. Loosen the edges and shake out onto a board. Cut in thick slices with a warm long knife.

Tomato and Parmesan Gratinée Tarts

Fall sees the abundance of plump, full-flavored plum tomatoes, which I enjoy serving pizza-style on disks of light, crisp pastry. The tomato slices are bound with melted Parmesan shavings and then placed on top of the pastry just before serving. A bouquet of arugula salad tops each tart. **SERVES 4 AS A FIRST COURSE**

10 ounces puff pastry, preferably homemade (page 214)

8 large, ripe plum tomatoes, skinned

2 tablespoons balsamic vinegar

2 tablespoons olive oil

1 tablespoon chopped fresh chervil

1 tablespoon chopped fresh parsley

2 ounces fresh Parmesan, shaved with a swivel peeler

4 ounces wild arugula

1–2 tablespoons Classic Vinaigrette (page 213)

Sea salt and freshly ground black pepper

1 Roll out the pastry to about ⅛-inch thickness. Cut out four rounds about 5 inches in diameter, using a saucer or small plate as a guide. Place on a heavy baking sheet and chill for 20 minutes.

2 Preheat the oven to 400°. Bake the pastry for 10 minutes, then place another baking sheet on top to press the rounds down and keep them flat. Bake for a further 8–10 minutes until just golden. Remove to a wire rack to cool and crisp.

3 Slice the tomatoes evenly and arrange on another baking sheet in four overlapping circles about the same size as the pastry rounds (certainly no larger). Brush with the balsamic vinegar and oil, season, and sprinkle with the herbs. Lay the shavings of Parmesan on top, making sure they connect with all the tomato slices – as they melt, the shavings will hold the tomato together.

4 Preheat the broiler. When really hot, place the tomatoes under the broiler near to the heat. The cheese should start to melt almost immediately. Watch carefully – the cheese doesn't need to brown much, just melt so it holds the tomato slices together.

5 Remove from the broiler and wait a few seconds, then using a slotted spatula transfer each round of tomato onto a pastry round.

6 Season the arugula and toss with the vinaigrette. Pile on top of each tart and serve.

Saffron Red Mullet on Vegetables à la Grecque

Red mullet, as you may have gathered, is one of my favorite foods. It not only tastes good, the thin red skin looks so inviting, and it gives me great scope to cook it in so many ways. If you cannot get red mullet, you can use pink or red bream instead. The fish is served on vegetables in a spicy oil marinade – a great casual main meal. The same idea works well with very fresh mackerel. Grelots are squat onions popular in France. Tubby shallots will do if you can't find them. **SERVES 4 AS A MAIN DISH**

4 small red mullets, about 8 ounces each,
  neatly filleted in two, skin on
5 tablespoons olive oil
2 generous pinches of saffron strands
4 bulbs baby fennel or 2 medium bulbs
2 medium carrots, thinly sliced
8 *grelot* onions or 4 fat shallots, sliced
Sea salt and freshly ground black pepper

Marinade
²/₃ cup olive oil
1 tablespoon white wine vinegar
1 tablespoon aged balsamic vinegar
6 coriander seeds, roughly crushed
6 white peppercorns, roughly crushed
1–4 star anise
4 whole cloves
6 sprigs fresh cilantro

1 Heat all the ingredients for the marinade until on the point of boiling, then set aside to infuse for 10–15 minutes.
2 Meanwhile, prepare the fish. Trim the fillets neatly, feeling for any pin bones with the tips of your fingers and pulling them out with tweezers or your fingernails. Rub both sides with 2 tablespoons of the olive oil and season. Crush the saffron strands on top of the pretty pink skin side. Set aside to marinate for 5–10 minutes.
3 If using baby fennel, trim and cut each in half lengthwise. If using larger bulbs, cut into quarters. Sauté the fennel in the remaining 3 tablespoons of olive oil for 3–5 minutes, then add the carrots and sauté for 2 minutes. Finally, add the onions (or shallots) and sauté for a further 2 minutes. Remove the vegetables to a shallow serving dish, season, and pour the marinade over. Leave to cool to room temperature.
4 Heat a large non-stick frying pan and, when you can feel a good heat rising, place the fish fillets in the pan, saffron-crusted-skin side down. Cook on this side for 5 minutes

until the flesh feels nearly firm and the skin is nice and crisp. Carefully flip the fillets over, taking care not to tear the skin, and cook the other side for just a minute or two. Season the fillets well.

5 Slip each cooked fillet gently into the dish and spoon the vegetables and marinade over to cover. Cool the fish to room temperature. Carefully pour off the marinade. (The marinade can be strained and stored in the fridge for up to a week to be used again.)

6 Serve the mullet fillets and marinated vegetables at room temperature or lightly chilled. This dish is good with a lightly dressed arugula salad.

Roasted Cod with Garlic Pomme Purée

Chunky cod with creamed potatoes is a culinary treasure, especially if cooked perfectly. Cod fillets from a fish 8½–11 pounds in weight give perfect texture – any larger and the flakes of flesh become too big and won't hold together after cooking. Did you know cod is the fish with the least amount of scales? This means the skin can be scored easily. We take advantage of this and insert cloutes *of herbs – thyme or rosemary sprigs or rolled-up basil leaves – through the skin. For the garlic potato, blanch and refresh the garlic cloves at least three times so you get the flavor without pungency.* **SERVES 4 AS A MAIN DISH**

2 large boiling potatoes

6 large cloves garlic

²/₃ cup milk

¼ cup heavy cream

5 tablespoons butter

4 ounces large fresh cèpes, trimmed and thinly sliced

Juice of ½ lemon

1 tablespoon olive oil

4 large *tranches* of cod (thick, neat pieces of fillet), 6–7 ounces each, skin on

Sea salt and freshly ground black pepper

1 Peel the potatoes and cut into even-size dice. Cook in boiling salted water for 12–15 minutes. Drain well, then return to the pan and dry out for 1–2 minutes over the heat. Mash the flesh or press through a potato ricer back into the pan.

2 While the potatoes are cooking, blanch the garlic in boiling water for a minute, then drain and refresh in cold water. Repeat the blanching twice more, then peel off the skin and mash the cloves to a purée on a small plate using a saucer. Mix into the potato.

3 Scald the milk and slowly stir into the potato purée with some seasoning. Then slowly add the cream to make a nice, velvety-smooth purée. Cook gently for 5 minutes, then gradually beat in half the butter, which has been cut into small dice.

4 Meanwhile, heat the remaining butter in a saucepan and gently fry the cèpes for about 4 minutes. Add the lemon juice and toss well until piping hot.

5 Heat the oil in a heavy-based frying pan and add the fish, skin-side down. Cook for 6–7 minutes until just firm, then flip the *tranches* over and cook briefly on the other side – 90% of the cooking time should be on the skin side.

6 To serve, place the *pomme purée* in the middle of four dinner plates, set the cod on top, and scatter the cèpes around.

Monkfish with Creamy Curried Mussels

This is a chunky, yet light and creamy main meal "soup," perfect for a blustery day when you'd like a dish of warming comfort food. The monkfish fillets are dusted in curry spices before roasting, which gives them an appetizing color and crust. **SERVES 4 AS A MAIN DISH**

1 large tail of monkfish, about 1 pound,
　filleted in two

8 ounces mussels

1 bay leaf

1 sprig fresh thyme

¼ cup dry white wine

1 carrot, finely diced

1 small leek, finely diced

1 small stalk celery, finely diced

2 tablespoons olive oil

2 teaspoons mild curry powder

2 pinches of saffron strands, crushed

1¼ cups Noilly Prat vermouth

1¼ cups Fish Stock (page 212)

1¼ cups heavy cream

4 ounces baby leaf spinach, shredded
　(about 1 cup)

Sea salt and freshly ground black pepper

1 Trim off as much of the gray membrane from the monkfish as possible. (It is important to do this so the fish does not curl during cooking.) Cut each fillet in half lengthwise so you have four fillets. Put into the fridge to chill.

2 Scrub the mussels and remove beards, if necessary. Discard any that don't close when tapped. Heat a large pan until very hot, then tip in the mussels with the thyme and wine. Clamp on the lid and cook for 3–4 minutes, shaking the pan once or twice. Uncover and discard any mussels that are still closed. Strain off the juices and reserve. Remove the mussel meat from the shells.

3 Sauté the diced carrot, leek, and celery (*mirepoix*) in 1 tablespoon of the oil for about 5 minutes until softened. Add 1 teaspoon of the curry powder and the saffron, and cook for a few seconds, then pour in the Noilly Prat. Cook until reduced down to a syrupy consistency. Add the stock and reserved mussel juices, and cook until reduced by half. Stir in the cream and simmer for 5 minutes. Season nicely and mix in the mussels and spinach. Reheat and keep the "soup" hot.

4 Dust the monkfish fillets with salt and the remaining curry powder. Heat the remaining oil in a non-stick frying pan and, when nice and hot, sear the fish in the hot oil, turning to brown evenly. Cook for 3–4 minutes on each side until the flesh firms enough to feel just lightly springy when pressed with the back of a fork. Season again. Remove and allow to rest for 3–4 minutes, then slice into medallions if you like.

5 Divide the "soup" among four warmed soup plates. Arrange the monkfish on top and serve.

John Dory with Ratatouille Vegetables and White Beans

We tend to think of eggplant, sweet peppers, and zucchini as early autumn vegetables – grown naturally, they are in abundance at this time of year. I "marry" them with some nicely cooked white beans, then serve with some pan-fried fillets of John Dory, which are best cooked skin on to hold them together. Porgy or other bream can also be used. The sauce is made with brown chicken stock. I often serve meat stocks with full-flavored fish. Incidentally, you can cook double or even triple the amount of beans and freeze what you don't use. It makes sound kitchen sense to cook a larger batch. SERVES 4 AS A MAIN DISH

1/2 cup dried haricot, navy, or other
  white beans, soaked overnight

1/2 small onion

1 small carrot, halved

2 sprigs fresh thyme

1 eggplant

2 medium zucchini

4 red sweet peppers

4 yellow sweet peppers

3 tablespoons olive oil

2 cups Dark Chicken Stock (page 212)

2/3 cup heavy cream

4 fillets of John Dory (or porgy or bream),
  about 4 ounces each, skin on

Sea salt and freshly ground black pepper

1 Drain the soaked beans and place in a pan of cold water. Bring to a boil and hold the boil for 10 minutes. Then drain and cover with fresh cold water. Add the onion, carrot, and 1 sprig of thyme. Bring to a boil, then simmer for 45–55 minutes until the beans are just tender but still whole. Drain, and discard the onion, carrot, and thyme. Season the beans as they cool.

2 Cut off the skin of the eggplant in 1/2-inch-thick lengths. You want nicely colored strips of vegetable, with skin. Discard the inner flesh or use it elsewhere. Cut the eggplant strips into triangles about 1 inch on all sides. Do the same with the zucchini.

3 Peel the skin from the whole peppers using a swivel vegetable peeler. Cut off the flesh in long pieces and discard the cores. Cut the pepper flesh into triangles, too.

4 Heat 2 tablespoons of the oil in a frying pan and gently sauté the eggplant pieces for about 3 minutes. Add the peppers and sauté for 2 minutes, then add the zucchini and sauté for a further 2–3 minutes. Season nicely. Ladle in about 1/2 cup of the stock, and add a few of the remaining thyme leaves. Simmer uncovered until the liquid reduces right down and coats the vegetables in a glossy glaze. Stir in the beans and reheat gently.

5 While the vegetables are cooking, boil the remaining stock until reduced by half. Add the cream and the last of the thyme leaves, and cook for 5 minutes. Season to taste.

6 Finally, heat the last of the oil in a large non-stick frying pan. Season the fish and cook it on the skin side for 3 minutes until nicely browned. Carefully turn the fillets over and cook the other side for 2 minutes or until just firm but still a little springy.

7 Divide the vegetables among four warmed plates, sit a fish fillet on top of each, and pour the sauce around.

Confit of Duck Legs

There's something very appealing about slow-cooked duck that is meltingly tender and falling away from the bone. The legs are particularly good cooked confit-style in goose fat, then served *with fries and a salad of curly endive. Use duck that is a little lean and full of flavor.*

SERVES 4 AS A MAIN DISH

Leaves from 1 sprig fresh thyme
4 duck legs
About 1 pound goose fat
1 fresh bouquet garni (bay leaf, few
   parsley stems, sprig fresh thyme, and
   a small stalk celery tied together)
8 ounces curly endive, separated into leaves
Classic Vinaigrette (page 213)
Fries (see My Special Steak Tartare
   and Fries, page 197), to serve
Sea salt and freshly ground black pepper

1 Press the leaves of fresh thyme onto the duck legs and sprinkle with sea salt. Leave at room temperature for 1 hour to draw out some moisture. In the meantime, preheat the oven to 325°.

2 Put the duck legs and goose fat in a pan and heat gently until just on the point of boiling. Transfer to a shallow casserole and add the bouquet garni. Cover and place in the oven. Slow roast for about 1½ hours until you can loosen the leg bone fairly easily. This indicates the meat is nicely tender.

3 Drain the legs and dab with paper towel. Strain the fat and keep for sautéeing potatoes and other uses – it is delicious. Heat a dry heavy-based frying pan and, when hot, cook the legs skin-side down for a few minutes to crisp the skin. Take care not to overcook.

4 Dress the curly endive with a little vinaigrette and place in the center of four plates. Arrange the fries around the edge, then place the crispy duck legs on top of the leaves.

Saddle of Rabbit with Herb Gnocchi

This is a good country dish served with style. Like duck, you can slow-cook rabbit in goose fat until the meat is deliciously tender. Once cooked, the meat can be served with homemade potato gnocchi and some oven-roasted tomatoes. A lovely, lazy lunch course.

SERVES 4 AS A MAIN DISH

2 rabbit tenderloins taken from a
  "saddle" weighing about 1 pound
1 tablespoon olive oil
Leaves from 1 sprig fresh rosemary, chopped
1 pound goose fat
Mixed salad leaves for garnish
Sea salt and freshly ground black pepper

Gnocchi
2 large boiling potatoes, about
  14 ounces each
About 1 cup all-purpose flour
1 teaspoon fine sea salt
1 extra large egg
1 tablespoon each chopped fresh basil
  and parsley
3–4 tablespoons olive oil

1 Wrap the rabbit tenderloins individually in plastic wrap and chill for 24 hours.

2 The next day, unwrap the tenderloins and rub lightly with the oil, then sprinkle the surface with a little salt and chopped rosemary leaves. Leave for 1 hour.

3 Place the rabbit and goose fat in a shallow heavy-based saucepan. Bring to a boil, then reduce the heat to the lowest possible setting. Cook for 1–1¼ hours, possibly more, until the meat is tender. Allow the rabbit to cool in the fat, then lift out and dab dry with paper towel. Keep the fat for other recipes.

4 While the rabbit is cooking, make the gnocchi. Preheat the oven to 350°. Bake the potatoes for about 1 hour until cooked. (Baking keeps the flesh dry.) Cool, then scoop out the flesh and mash or press through a potato ricer. Mix with the flour, salt, egg, and herbs. Gradually work in 3 tablespoons of the oil until you have a firm, but still soft dough.

5 Turn out onto a cold floured surface and knead gently until smooth. Roll into long cigar shapes, wrap in plastic wrap, and allow to rest and cool.

6 Bring a large pan of salted water to a boil and add the remaining oil. Using the back of a table knife (this helps to squash the ends to a traditional gnocchi shape), cut off 1¼-inch lengths. (See photographs of this technique on page 220.) Drop straight into the simmering water and cook for about 3 minutes.

7 Have ready a large bowl of ice water. As each batch of gnocchi is cooked, lift out with a slotted spoon and dunk straight into the ice water. Leave for a minute or so, then drain well and pat dry with a paper towel.

8 When ready to serve, preheat the broiler. When it is hot, brown the rabbit tenderloins lightly on all sides. Meanwhile, heat some oil or goose fat in a frying pan and fry the cooked gnocchi for 3–4 minutes until crisp on both sides. Drain on paper towels.

9 Cut each rabbit tenderloin diagonally in half and serve with the potato gnocchi and a mixed salad leaf garnish.

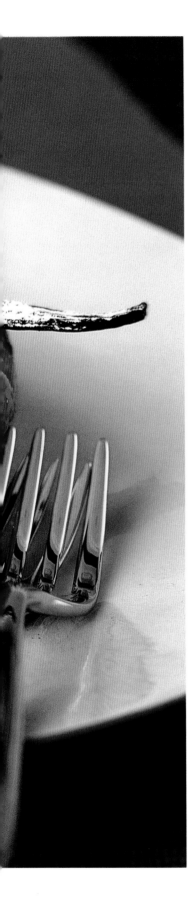

Caramelized Apple Tart

Making a fruit tart with crisp pastry and tender fruit can be tricky. The answer is to bake it upside down, so the fruit juices do not leach into the pastry and make it soggy. Ideally, make this tart in a shallow metal pan that will go into the oven, such as a gratin pan, paella pan, or proper tarte Tatin mold (in the restaurant, we make individual tarts and decorate with a slit vanilla bean dusted with confectioners' sugar). Serve with some scoops of a rich vanilla ice cream, or try homemade Thyme Ice Cream (page 214), Fromage Blanc Sorbet (page 215), Lemon Sorbet (page 215), or quenelles of mascarpone. **SERVES 2–3**

3 large pippin apples
10 ounces puff pastry, preferably homemade (page 214)
3 tablespoons cold unsalted butter, thinly sliced
¹⁄₂ cup sugar mixed with ¹⁄₄ teaspoon Chinese
   five-spice powder

1 About 4 hours before cooking, quarter the apples, cut out the core, and peel thinly. Leave the apple quarters uncovered so they oxidize a little and dry out. It doesn't matter if they brown because, of course, they will be coated in a caramel anyway.
2 Roll out the pastry and cut out a circle 9–9¹⁄₂ inches in diameter (this is assuming you will be making a tart of 8–8¹⁄₂ inches diameter). You may find it helpful to use a large round cake pan as a template. Prick lightly with the tip of a sharp knife and chill for an hour or two.
3 Preheat the oven to 400°. When ready to cook, layer the thinly sliced hard butter in the bottom of your pan and sprinkle the spiced sugar over. Press the apple quarters into the butter, cored side uppermost, arranging them in a circle with one in the center.
4 Place the pan over a medium heat. After a few minutes, start to roll the pan so the butter and sugar dissolve and mix together. Tip the pan occasionally so you can check that the caramel is forming. Cook like this for a total of 10 minutes, then remove from the heat.
5 Lay the pastry over the pan and tuck the edges down inside, pressing in with a fork. Place the pan in the oven (take care because the caramel will be hot and could dribble down your arm – you must avoid chef's arms!). Bake for about 15 minutes until the pastry is golden brown and crisp. Remove and cool before up-ending onto a large round platter. If the caramel sticks fast, then reheat it for a few minutes to melt.

Pear, Honey, and Lime Cake

I do enjoy homey cakes, and this is becoming a favorite with my family. It's a combination of a traditional English sponge cake and a French tarte bourdaloue. *Eat it as a teatime treat, or serve warm with cream for dessert.* **SERVES 6**

4 tablespoons unsalted butter

3 Comice pears, peeled, halved, and cored

1/3 cup light flower-scented honey

Grated zest and juice of 2 limes

1 vanilla bean

1/2 cup pear *eau-de-vie*

Cake

3/4 cup (1 1/2 sticks) unsalted butter, softened to room temperature

1 1/2 cups + 2 tablespoons sugar

1 teaspoon baking powder

1/8 teaspoon salt

4 extra large eggs, beaten

1 1/2 cups cake flour, sifted

1 Melt the 4 tablespoons of butter in a shallow pan and cook the pears for about 5 minutes until they take on a light golden color, turning once or twice. Stir in the honey, lime juice, and vanilla bean. Cook for a further 2 minutes or so, then stir in the *eau-de-vie*. Remove from the heat and leave the pears to steep in the syrup until cool, about 3 hours.

2 To make the cake batter, beat the butter and sugar with the lime zest until smooth, then mix in the baking powder and salt. Gradually work in the beaten eggs, then, using a large metal spoon, fold in the sifted flour. Cover the bowl with plastic wrap and set aside to rest for 45 minutes.

3 When ready to bake, preheat the oven to 400°. Grease and line a 9-inch round cake pan that is about 2 1/2 inches deep.

4 Drain the pears and pat lightly dry. Reserve the syrup. Slash 3 of the halves evenly into slices, keeping them attached at the thin end in the shape of pear halves. Chop the remaining pears and stir into the cake batter. Spoon the cake batter into the pan, level the top, and place the slashed pear halves on top.

5 Bake for 10 minutes. Reduce the oven temperature to 300°, and continue baking for 45–50 minutes until the top of the cake feels lightly springy. Test if it is cooked by pushing a long thin wooden stick into the center; it should come out clean. Leave the cake to cool for 15 minutes in the pan, then unmold onto a wire rack and cool completely.

6 If liked, skewer the cake a few times and spoon 4–6 tablespoons of the pear syrup over. Brush the top of the slashed pears with some syrup before serving.

Pear and Frangipane Tart

This classic dessert is always popular, and, more to the point, easy to make. I always roll out far more pastry than is needed to line the pan, to allow for shrinkage. This way the filling can be completely level with the top of the pastry shell, with no dips or gaps. Serve warm with crème fraîche or a trickle of heavy cream. **SERVES 6**

3 even-size firm pears (such as
  Bartlett or Comice)
2½ cups Stock Syrup (page 214)
1 vanilla bean, slit open

Pastry
½ cup (1 stick) unsalted butter, softened
  to room temperature
5 tablespoons granulated sugar
1 vanilla bean
1 large egg, beaten
1⅓ cups all-purpose flour sifted with
  ⅛ teaspoon fine sea salt

Filling
1⅓ cups ground almonds
½ cup granulated sugar
7 tablespoons unsalted butter
2½ tablespoons flour
2 extra large eggs, beaten
2 tablespoons dark rum
A little confectioners' sugar infused
  with 1 sprig fresh rosemary

1 First, poach the pears. Peel thinly, halve, and core. Bring the stock syrup to a boil, add the vanilla, and then slip in the pears. Turn the heat down and poach gently for 10–12 minutes until softened. Remove, drain, and cool. (The syrup can be strained, cooled, and chilled for re-use.)

2 Now, make the pastry. Beat the butter with the sugar until smooth and creamy. Slit the vanilla bean and scrape out the seeds with the tip of a sharp knife. Add to the mixture. Work in the beaten egg and flour alternately until you have a smooth dough. Knead lightly, then wrap in plastic wrap and chill for 20 minutes or so.

3 Roll out the dough as thinly as you are able, to a round about 12 inches in diameter, large enough to line an 8½-inch tart pan, about 1–1¼ inches deep, comfortably with overhang. You could do this on a lightly floured board, or between two lightly floured sheets of plastic wrap. Lift the dough on the rolling pin into the tart pan (or a flan ring set on a heavy, flat baking sheet). Press the dough well onto the bottom and sides of the pan, and pinch together or patch any gaps with dough trimmings. Don't trim off overhang. Place the pan on a baking sheet.

4 Fit a large sheet of foil into the pastry shell, bringing it well up the sides. Fill with baking beans. Chill again for 20 minutes, while you preheat the oven to 350°.

5 Bake the pastry shell for 15 minutes. Remove the foil and beans, and bake for 5 more minutes. Trim the top of the pastry shell level with the pan using a sharp knife, then set aside.

6 Place all the filling ingredients (except the rosemary-infused confectioners' sugar) into a food processor and blend until smooth and creamy. Spoon into the pastry shell and level the top. Press the drained pears lightly on the surface in a circle, rounded side up. Bake for 35–40 minutes until the filling is firm and springs back when pressed on top. Cool until warm.

7 Serve in wedges dusted with rosemary-infused confectioners' sugar.

Creamed Sweet Rice with Autumn Fruits

I make no excuses – this is a rich dessert, but worth every sweet, creamy mouthful. Serve it warm or cold (when it can be shaped into scoops or quenelles). The fruits add a good contrast in color and flavor. **SERVES 4–6**

3 large red plums, pitted and sliced
1 large pear, peeled, cored, and sliced
2 tablespoons confectioners' sugar
½ cup Stock Syrup (page 214) or apple cider
1 cup blackberries
1 vanilla bean
1¼ cups whole milk
1¼ cups heavy cream
¾ cup short-grain rice
6 egg yolks
¾ cup granulated sugar

1 Roast the fruits first. Get a clean non-stick frying pan really hot. Toss the plums and pear in the confectioners' sugar, then cook briefly in the hot pan until they start to caramelize. This will take a couple of minutes. Remove and mix with the stock syrup or cider and the blackberries. Set aside to cool.

2 Slit the vanilla bean lengthwise and, using the tip of a sharp knife, scrape out the seeds. Add these and the vanilla bean to the milk and cream in a heavy-based saucepan. Bring slowly to scalding point, when the liquid should start to rise up the sides of the pan.

3 Stir in the rice and return to a boil, stirring occasionally. Simmer gently, uncovered, for about 20 minutes until the rice is soft and most of the liquid absorbed.

4 Beat the egg yolks and granulated sugar until creamy and smooth in a large heatproof bowl, placed on a damp cloth to hold it steady. Gradually mix in the hot rice, beating well. Return it all to the pan and stir over a very gentle heat until it starts to thicken, about 5 minutes. Do not let the pudding overheat or it will curdle. Cool, stirring occasionally to stop a skin from forming. (We cool our pudding down rapidly over a bowl of crushed ice.)

5 Serve warm or cold, with the fruits and a little of their syrup spooned over.

winter

Surprisingly, winter can be a very good season for a variety of foods. Roots and crucifers are in prime condition, a lot of game is in high season, and fish from icy waters is plump and full of flavor. And now that air transport is so fast and efficient, we can obtain wonderful quality fresh fruits and vegetables from the southern hemisphere. So we can really have the best of both worlds.

Frosty conditions may wilt some vegetables, but it seems to make certain hardy greens such as **cabbage** and sprouts more spriggy. My favorite cabbages are the Savoy and napa cabbage. Obligingly, both remain crisp and fresh for several days in the fridge. The dark green, outer leaves of Savoy cabbage we use for wrapping up small, tightly packed balls of shredded braised oxtail or *confit* of duck. We also like to dry the large outer leaves, to use as a crisp garnish for sweetbreads. To prepare this, the leaves are sautéed whole, then packed between metal baking sheets lined with parchment paper and baked at the lowest oven temperature for about 45 minutes. Napa cabbage is wonderful with braised and poached fish. We shred the leaves finely into julienne strips, sauté them in butter with tips of thyme, and then ladle in a little chicken stock just to moisten. This can be done ahead for reheating at the last moment.

Another good leafy-cum-stem vegetable for the winter months is **Swiss chard**, which I like to call by its French name *blette*. The two parts are prepared separately, with the leafy tops treated like spinach and the ribbed stems like celery. They often need a light peeling before being cut into *bâtons* and sautéed. Chard is good with game. I also like to serve it with roasted bass with a vanilla-flavored butter sauce (one of my first hallmark dishes at the Aubergine).

The Scots are very partial to **rutabaga** – I have many happy memories of my Mum's buttery golden purée – and they are popular in many other parts of the world. In France, however, rutabaga and other root vegetables were traditionally fed to the pigs. We may laugh at this, but I dare say the French could wag their fingers at us about our attitudes to celeriac and beets. The lightly sweet, slightly musky flavor of rutabaga suits game birds such as pan-fried squab and roast guinea fowl as well as full-flavored fish – I once tried it very successfully with a fillet of zander, a pike-perch type of fish popular in Europe. We cook rutabaga in buttery stock first, then blend it until smooth and return the purée to the heat to dry off a little. Rutabaga has enough body to stand on its own as a purée and doesn't need any potato with it.

The strange-looking **kohlrabi** may be a subject of curiosity for many of us, but take my word for it – the flavor cannot be matched by any other root vegetable. It resembles a turnip, but is sweeter and more delicate. I think kohlrabi is best diced and sautéed in oil and butter before being braised with a little chicken stock until just tender. Like this it's good with light game, and it makes a light creamy soup too.

We tend to take large **"old" potatoes** for granted, tossing big bags into the supermarket cart without looking at the label. But if you take time to check the variety, you can select potatoes with a fine flavor or those suitable for particular uses such as roasting or baking. I think it's worth paying a few extra cents per pound for the best – after all, a good potato is still the best value food. If you want to make mind-blowing mash, try baking the potatoes first, unpeeled, on a bed of rock salt. When soft, halve, scoop out the flesh, and mash until smooth. Mix in softly whipped cream and a large pat of best butter, and season nicely too – bland mash is a big disappointment. I like to serve chunky fries with steak tartare and – another example of the humble potato becoming a gourmet's delight – I make a simple creamy potato soup very special by stirring in fine shreds of black truffle.

A winter vegetable appreciated by many chefs is **salsify** (see photograph on page 165). Home cooks are beginning to discover its joys too. The weird, dark, thin, cigar-shaped roots do look a little uninviting, but peel them thinly and underneath you will find pale cream flesh that looks similar to white asparagus. Salsify has a tremendous flavor – robust and strong. Once peeled, it needs to be dunked into lemony water because it browns quickly. After a blanch in boiling water, you can cut the stems into thin lozenge shapes and sauté them in olive oil

and butter until lightly browned. Salsify is fantastic with duck, veal, and, especially, firm flatfish.

Although on sale almost all the year round, leeks are most associated with winter dishes. In fact, leeks are best in the winter, before the inner cores harden, and we don't waste any part of them. The large outer leaves have a number of uses in our kitchen. The tougher ones act as wraps for bouquets garnis, while large inner leaves are turned into an attractive garnish: we shred them very finely and deep-fry, then crisp up in a low oven, ruffling through the shreds as they dry out to make them a bit "bouffant." We *confit* slim *bâtons* of inner leek (and baby leeks too) in goose fat for about 8 minutes, then drain and broil until crisp on the outside. Leeks marry well with most other flavors, but I particularly like to sprinkle a pinch or two of crushed saffron strands over them as they braise in buttery stock or simmer in a leek soup. Whole baby leeks are great blanched and served with a lemon butter sauce.

If you are looking for some unusual vegetable chips, then try leek leaves. Split open the white of a leek and cut the layers into large bite-size squares. Blanch to soften, then pat dry and brush each side with truffle oil. Dry them out in a very low oven until crisp. They'll be a sure talking point at any party, I promise.

Some vegetables have a foot in both camps – hot and cold. One of these is Belgian endive. Although most commonly used as a salad vegetable, in my kitchen we usually serve them cooked. They are best caramelized first in hot oil with sugar, salt, and a touch or two of Chinese five-spice. After this they can be moistened with fresh orange juice and a little chicken stock, covered with a butter wrapper, and braised in a medium hot oven for about 15 minutes until tender but not soft. Braised endive is great with fish, chicken, and rabbit. I also like to make chicory "fans" (make them like the fennel fans on page 136).

Where would any chef worth his or her salt be without their *lentilles de Puy*? In France, where they come from, they even have their own A.C. (*appellation contrôlée*). The uses for the lentils from Le Puy are almost endless. They're fantastic in soups, like our well-known "cappuccino" of lentils with langoustines; great mixed with a fine *brunoise* of carrots, celery, and onions as a "garnish" for lamb; and wonderful tossed with vinaigrette to serve with squab. Marcus Wareing, my head chef at Petrus, in London, has an imaginative way of serving lentils with braised onion petals flavored with truffle oil. We also use a fine purée of lentils as a thickener in soups and velouté sauces, although it does darken the color somewhat. If you can't get *lentilles de Puy*, the larger greeny lentils are a reasonable substitute.

There is certainly an art to shucking an oyster, and once you have mastered it you must then fine tune it with lots of practice! (The other two marks of a good chef are filleting a sea bass and "turning" an artichoke.) You must never try to open an oyster from the side, it must be from the hinge at the top. Wrap your hand in several layers of thick dish towel, and cup an oyster with the flat shell uppermost. Take a firm, stubby knife with a good point (the classic oyster knife, if possible) and stick it in firmly, but not violently, at the hinge end. Wiggle the knife a little from side to side, and you should suddenly feel a "give" as the hinge muscle is cut. Push the knife tip in a bit further and twist to lift up the shell. Inside is the oyster and juice. Be sure to save the juice. Slip the knife under the oyster to release the muscle, and that's it. A good oyster-opener leaves no bits of shell inside, although a novice will be excused the occasional bit. The essence of shucking is not speed but care. If we cook oysters at all, we just poach them in their own juice with a little *nage* and a couple of whole star anise. The smoky aromatic flavors blend sublimely. European flat oysters, which are in season during the winter, are more tricky to open than Pacific oysters, with their craggy shells.

There are many fishes more often associated with winter than warmer days. The first that comes to mind for most people is cod. Maybe that's because roasted and served with creamy mash, it's the ultimate comfort food. I associate cod with winter because that is when I used to go line fishing for it off a western Scottish beach with my dad. I think we were entrants in the White Horse whisky fishing championships. Anyway, although it is a great feeling to catch a big fish, from a cooking point of view, any fish that is over 11 pounds will be too flaky to hold together in the pan. The flakes are just too meaty, although the flavor is still fantastic. Instead, in the kitchen we like to cook smaller codlings around $3\frac{1}{2}$–$6\frac{1}{2}$ pounds. Once filleted, the best way to cook cod is skin-side down in a really hot pan, so the skin becomes crisp. Then serve with a garlicky *pomme purée* or a vinaigrette of *lentilles de Puy*. (Incidentally, when you cook cod skin, do check that the fine small scales have been rubbed off. It's not often the case.)

In top European restaurants, brill is becoming as popular as turbot. It's a strong fish, so can take a red wine marinade and full-bodied sauces made with chicken or veal stock, yet it still retains a fine tender texture when eaten. Brill are generally longer than turbots, but when they are small it is hard to tell them apart. If you buy a whole fish, turn it upside down and look for the "oysters" by the jaw bone. Fillet them out with a sharp knife and pan-fry like scallops – they are a good cook's treat, or a garnish should you feel generous and want to share them. Brill bones make wonderful fish stock because they are quite gelatinous. Roast the brill bones first, as you would do meat bones, then cook in a red wine stock with strips of smoky bacon.

Red meats are a natural for winter dishes, and we are finding people are increasingly willing to try venison. Our venison is farmed on an estate in Aberdeenshire, Scotland, where the deer are allowed to roam almost at will, so they are virtually free-range. The meat is hung for 2–3 weeks. After butchering, we marinate it in a neutral oil like peanut with crushed juniper berries and fresh rosemary for at least 7 days. This opens up the muscle fibers and makes the meat really tender. We sometimes roast the loins and serve with rounds of fresh beet cooked fondant-style, in a little stock. Another favorite way of serving is with a garnish of chopped cabbage, turnip, and carrot all braised together and then bound with a little cream. Slices of just pink venison are laid on top and covered with a red wine sauce enriched with a bit of dark chocolate. The flavor intrigues our diners. A few fresh raspberries on top completes the elegant presentation.

Pork doesn't appear much on my menus, yet it is a meat that I think is perfect for serving home-cooked on chilly winter days. I love it with cabbage flavored with a few pods of cardamom. The main way we use pork is pig's feet. My restaurant is on the site of what was Pierre Koffman's renowned Tante Claire in London. As I was once Pierre's head chef, this is a significant honor for me. Pierre's genius gave London many great dishes, but perhaps his best known were *pieds de cochon*, or stuffed pig's feet. His most famous was a stuffing of sweetbreads and morels. My recipe for pig's feet (which you will find on page 199) is really posh bacon and eggs. Topped with fried quail eggs and shavings of white truffle, I serve it as an *amuse-gueule*. Pig's feet are very gelatinous and the thick, flavorsome braising liquid is a favorite staff lunch.

Another animal extremity that makes very fine eating is oxtail. After an unnecessary (to my mind at least) ban of beef on the bone in the U.K., we are now able to restore this classic casserole to pride of place on our winter menus. We stew oxtail gently in red wine with root vegetables, stock, and a hint of spice. When the meat is very tender, it is pulled into shreds and bound in a ball with thin *crepine* or set in a terrine to be served in slices with a salad of lentils in mustard vinaigrette. Butchers sell oxtails cut neatly into disks and bound with string. For a simpler serving, you could simply cook them as a normal rich beef stew, but do try to take time to remove the meat from the bone before serving.

Two fruits brighten up the long, cold winter days for me (not that we see much daylight in our kitchen). These are pineapples and citrus fruits. Large sweet pineapples come from the tropics and travel well. You can check their ripeness by pulling out a green leaf at the top – just a tug should do it. We use pineapple in *tarte Tatins*, compotes, and sorbets, and to make terrific *tuiles*. For a light dessert, blend the flesh with a caramel sauce, and top with creamy yogurt and shavings of a fruit granita.

Oranges, lemons, and limes are the fruits we most associate with winter, which is strange considering they don't grow in our cold British climate. But they do travel and store well, and we are certainly grateful for them. Blood oranges and pink grapefruit are the two citrus fruits I like to feature when they come into season – blood oranges for their rich color and startling flavor, and pink grapefruit because they break down into the prettiest little tear shapes. These we mix into a vinaigrette and serve with a warm salad of red mullet or poached Scottish lobster with fresh cilantro.

One of our most refreshing desserts is a terrine of sliced citrus fruits with a tangy lemon sorbet. We also soak slices of lemon in stock syrup to make a sweet *confit*, and press them onto fillets of fish or sweetbreads before pan-roasting and serving with harissa-flavored couscous. The same can be done with lime slices, and cooked with squab breasts. Limes also feature as the tangy flavor in guacamole and in honey syrups for poaching all kinds of fruit.

Velouté of Cauliflower with a Brunoise of Scallops

This light cream soup has a velvety texture created by cooking tiny cauliflower florets in milk. To finish, add some finely diced fresh scallops, which cook almost instantly in the hot liquid. This soup is nicest served in elegant small teacups. **SERVES 4 AS A FIRST COURSE**

1 medium head cauliflower
1 tablespoon butter
1 cup milk
1 cup Light Chicken Stock (page 212)
  or Fish Stock (page 212)
1/2 cup heavy cream
4 medium scallops, shucked,
  without corals
Tiny pinches of cayenne pepper
Sea salt and freshly ground black pepper

1 Cut the cauliflower into florets. Discard the stems (or save them for another use). Heat the butter in a saucepan, stir in the cauliflower florets, and gently sweat for up to 10 minutes, stirring occasionally.
2 Pour in the milk and add seasoning. Continue cooking gently for 5 minutes, then add the stock. Return to a simmer, partially cover the pan, and cook until the florets are very soft, about 15 minutes. You should be able to press them gently against the side of the pan to crush. There is no need to blend in a processor.
3 Add the cream and cook for a few minutes longer. Check the seasoning.
4 Now, cut the scallops into small dice – what chefs call a *brunoise*. Divide this among four small soup cups or teacups. Season and dust with tiny pinches of cayenne.
5 Return the soup to a boil and pour over the scallops. Don't stir – the scallops should be a surprise! Eat soon.

Creamy Potato Soup with Parsley Chantilly

This soup is made in a somewhat different way from the traditional "sweat veg, add stock, and blend to a purée" recipe. For a start, instead of boiling the potatoes, they are baked. The variety of potato is important. I use the golden-fleshed, well-flavored Ratte because, despite its waxy texture, it has a lot of starch. Yukon Gold potatoes are similar. I use a brown chicken stock to give the soup a country color, and finish with stunning whipped cream and parsley floats.

SERVES 4 AS A FIRST COURSE

About 1 cup parsley sprigs (no stems)
3 cloves garlic
Some rock salt for baking
10 ounces potatoes, washed
1 shallot, minced
1 tablespoon olive oil
1 sprig fresh thyme
2 cups Dark Chicken Stock (page 212)
½ cup heavy cream
Sea salt and freshly ground black pepper

1 Blanch the parsley sprigs in boiling water for 2 minutes, then drain in a colander and refresh under cold running water. Drain again and place in a clean dish towel. Wring the towel hard to extract the liquid. Purée the parsley in a food processor or, if you don't have one that can cope with such small quantities, mince the parsley very finely. Set aside.

2 Blanch the garlic in boiling water to cover for 30 seconds. Drain and blanch again. If you can bear it, repeat this a third time. This helps to remove the pungency of garlic, yet retains the flavor. Drain and mince the garlic.

3 Preheat the oven to 350°. Sprinkle the bottom of a small roasting pan with rock salt and roll the wet potatoes in it. Bake for about 45 minutes until the flesh feels soft when pierced with a sharp knife. Cool until just comfortable enough to hold. (We wear rubber gloves for the next stage.) Peel the hot potatoes, then rub through a sieve with a ladle or push through a potato ricer. Set aside.

4 Sauté the shallot in the oil with the thyme for 5 minutes until soft. Mix in the potato and crushed garlic, and cook for a minute or two. Gradually stir in the stock as you would when making a risotto. This helps to keep the texture of the soup smooth and velvety. Season and bring to a boil. That's the soup made.

5 Now for the parsley *Chantilly*. Whip the cream until it holds its shape, season, and fold in the parsley purée.

6 Serve the soup in bowls with the cream on top in soft dollops or more formal quenelles.

Fennel Soup with Baby Clams

If you cook clams like mussels, until the shells open, you can lift out the flesh very easily. Save the juice for the soup – it adds to the flavor. **SERVES 4 AS A FIRST COURSE**

8 ounces live baby clams,
 purged if necessary
½ cup dry white wine
1 sprig fresh thyme
1 bay leaf
4 medium bulbs fennel
1 tablespoon butter
1 tablespoon olive oil
1 onion, chopped
4 leaves fresh basil, chopped

2 tablespoons Pernod
4 cups Fish Stock (page 212)
1 cup heavy cream
Sea salt and freshly ground black pepper

Curry oil (optional)
3 tablespoons olive oil
1 teaspoon mild curry powder

1 First, cook the clams. Heat an empty saucepan until very hot, then tip in the clams, wine, thyme, and bay leaf. Clamp on the lid and cook for about 5 minutes. Discard any clams that have not opened. Strain the juice and reserve. Pick out the meat from the shells and set aside.

2 Slice the base from the fennel bulbs and discard, then pull the segments apart. Slice them thinly lengthwise into fine julienne strips.

3 Heat the butter and oil in a large saucepan and sauté the fennel strips and onion for about 10 minutes, stirring occasionally, until softened. Add the chopped basil and continue cooking for 2 minutes. Deglaze with the Pernod and cook for 1 minute, then pour in the fish stock and clam juice. Bring to a boil, season nicely, and simmer for 15 minutes.

4 Meanwhile, for the optional curry oil garnish, heat the oil with the curry powder, stirring. When sizzling, remove from the heat and set aside.

5 Pass the soup through a fairly open sieve or colander so you keep some texture. Return to the pan, stir in the cream, and check the seasoning. Bring back to a boil.

6 Divide the clams among four warmed soup bowls and ladle the just boiling soup over. This will be enough to reheat the cooked clams. Add a trickle of curry oil, if using, and serve.

Smoked Haddock and Mustard Chowder

In Scotland, they call a thick haddock and potato soup like this Cullen Skink, but I call this recipe a chowder so you all know what to expect. Do try to use natural undyed smoked haddock. My French training tempted me to add some coarsegrain French mustard, to celebrate the "auld alliance." For a smart garnish, boil 4 quail eggs for 2½ minutes, then peel and halve. Set on the soup just before serving. **SERVES 4 AS A FIRST COURSE**

1 large undyed smoked haddock fillet (finnan haddie), about 1 pound
2 cups milk
2 large boiling potatoes,
   about 10 ounces each
2 tablespoons olive oil
1 large shallot, chopped
½ cup dry white wine
2 cups Fish Stock (page 212)
6 tablespoons heavy cream
1 heaped tablespoon coarsegrain mustard
Sea salt and freshly ground black pepper

1 Cut the haddock fillet in two or three pieces to fit into a large saucepan. Bring the milk to a boil in the saucepan, then slip in the "haddie" fillet. Remove the pan from the heat and leave for about 10 minutes. By then the fish will feel firm when pressed.

2 Lift out the fish, then strain the milk and reserve. Skin and flake the fish while still warm. Set aside.

3 Peel the potatoes and cut into small dice. Heat the oil and sauté the potatoes with the shallot for about 10 minutes, stirring occasionally, until lightly colored. Add the wine and cook until reduced right down, then pour in the stock and reserved milk. Season and bring to a boil, stirring once or twice. Simmer for 15 minutes until the potatoes feel just tender.

4 Blend the mixture until smooth, either in the pan with an immersion blender or decanted into a food processor or blender.

5 Return to the pan, if necessary, and stir in the cream. Briskly stir in the mustard and check the seasoning again. Gradually stir in the flaked haddie, reheat gently, and serve.

Salt Cod Pâté with Cherry Tomato Dressing

Salt cod is a popular ingredient in many parts of the world, from the Mediterranean to the West Indies (for reasons historical). Salting the flesh of cod concentrates the flavor and firms the texture. The Spanish, Portuguese, and French all have wonderful recipes for flaked salt cod and creamed potato, shaping the mixture into fritters or brandades. *Salt cod can be bought in various grades and strengths, but it is easy to make yourself and requires only 24 hours advance salting. So, let's start with that. Incidentally, freshly made salt cod has many other uses, so you might consider making double the quantity. Once lightly poached and flaked, you can use it in fish cakes or serve it with a cream of parsley sauce. The pâté is a great party dish, and the cherry tomato dressing can also be used as a light dip for crudités and croûtes cut from* ficelles *(small baguettes).* **SERVES 4 AS A FIRST COURSE**

10-ounce fillet of cod
½ cup coarse sea salt
A few fresh parsley stems, twisted
2 large pinches of curry powder
1 tablespoon olive oil
1 medium boiling potato,
   peeled and diced
1¼ cups milk
1 fat clove garlic, minced
1 tablespoon chopped fresh parsley
½ cup heavy cream
Sea salt and freshly ground black pepper

Dressing
8 ounces sun-ripened
   cherry tomatoes
½ teaspoon sugar
7 tablespoons peanut or olive oil,
   plus extra for drizzling
1 tablespoon Dijon mustard

1 Lay the cod in a shallow dish and sprinkle the salt and parsley stems over. Cover the fish with plastic wrap, then press a heavy plate on top. Chill for 24 hours, turning once, by which time you will find liquid oozing out and the fish firmed up.

2 Drain, rinse in cold water, and pat dry. Discard the parsley stems. The cod fillet should now weigh about 7 ounces.

3 Cut the cod into large chunks and dust with curry powder. Heat the oil in a non-stick frying pan and sauté the cod until a good golden brown and quite firm. It is best overcooked slightly. Drain, cool, and flake. Set aside.

4 Cook the potato in the milk with the minced garlic and seasoning. Drain well, reserving some of the milk. Blend to a purée in a food processor (one of the few times when I do this!). If the mixture is a bit thick, trickle in some of the saved milk.

5 Cool the potato, then mix in the flaked cod and parsley. Whip the cream until it holds soft peaks. Fold into the cod mixture. Check the seasoning. Chill the mixture in a bowl if you wish to shape it into quenelles, or just press into ramekins and mark the top with the tip of a knife or prongs of a fork.

6 For the dressing, blend the tomatoes to a purée in a food processor. Press the purée through a
sieve into a bowl, rubbing with the back of a ladle. Mix in the sugar, oil, mustard, and seasoning.
That's it. There is no need for any vinegar as the tomatoes are acid enough. (This makes scant
1 cup, which leaves plenty of extra dressing to serve with crudités.)

7 If serving the pâté in a bowl or ramekins, you can make a hollow in the center and fill with
some of the fresh tomato dressing, or trickle it over the top with a little extra olive oil.
Another suggestion is to spread the pâté thickly on croûtes, sprinkle with freshly grated
Parmesan, and broil until lightly browned.

Seafood in a Nage with Carrot Spaghetti

This is my version of a plat de fruits de mer *– a glorious collection of favorite seafood served in a light aromatic vegetable broth scented with star anise. It is served with a thin "spaghetti" of carrots, which can be cut on a razor-sharp mandoline or food processor attachment.*

SERVES 4 AS A MAIN DISH

2 carrots
5 tablespoons butter
2 cups Vegetable *Nage* (page 212),
    plus 3 tablespoons
3 star anise
5 ounces live baby clams
3 tablespoons dry white wine
8 live oysters
4 sea scallops, shucked,
    without corals
2 tablespoons heavy cream
A good squeeze of lemon juice
1 heaped tablespoon shredded fresh basil
Sea salt and freshly ground black pepper

1 First, cut the carrots into long, thin "spaghetti" using a mandoline, Japanese slicer, or an equivalent slicer blade on a food processor. Bring the butter and the 3 tablespoons of *nage* to a boil. Stir in the carrot spaghetti, season, and cover. Cook for 1 minute, then set aside.

2 Heat the rest of the *nage* until boiling. Add the star anise, then remove from the heat and infuse for 10 minutes. Discard the anise.

3 Heat a large saucepan and, when hot, add the clams and wine. Clamp on the lid and cook for 3–5 minutes, shaking the pan occasionally, until the shells open. Discard any clams whose shells remain steadfastly shut. Pick the meat from the shells and set aside. Strain and save the juice.

4 Shuck the oysters, saving the juice (if the fish merchant does this, be sure to ask him to save the juice). Cut each scallop horizontally in three.

5 Reheat the *nage* and slip in the slices of scallops. Heat on a bare simmer, then add the oysters and cook for 1 minute. Finally, drop in the shelled clams. Stir in the saved juices too. Check the seasoning, and stir in the cream, lemon juice, and basil.

6 As soon as everything is hot, divide the seafood among four soup bowls and ladle the hot stock over. Top with the carrot spaghetti and serve.

Brill in Red Wine with Beurre Rouge

You may find it strange cooking white fish in red wine, but it works really well and looks so attractive when you cut into the fillet. The sauce, called a beurre rouge, *is made by reducing the liquid down and whisking in butter. Vegetable accompaniments include potato purée, butter-glazed* grelot *onions (or baby shallots), and salsify.* SERVES 4 AS A MAIN DISH

1 pound boiling potatoes

⅓ cup heavy cream

11 tablespoons butter

5 ounces salsify

A large squeeze of lemon juice

3 tablespoons olive oil

12 *grelot* onions, peeled

1 large shallot, minced

2 cups red wine

2 cups Fish Stock (page 212)

4 fillets of brill (or sole or flounder), about 5 ounces each

1 tablespoon chopped fresh parsley

Sea salt and fresh ground black pepper

1 Cook the potatoes, in their skins, in boiling salted water for 12–15 minutes until tender, then drain. Peel while hot (wear rubber gloves), then mash or press through a potato ricer back into the pan. Heat for a minute or two, then beat in 3 tablespoons of the cream and 2 tablespoons of the butter until thick and creamy. Season and set aside.

2 Peel the salsify with a swivel peeler, then rinse well and slice diagonally into thin *bâtons*. Blanch in boiling water with the lemon juice for 2 minutes, then drain and cool.

3 Heat 2 tablespoons of the oil and, when hot, sauté the onions for about 5 minutes, turning frequently. Pat the salsify dry, then add to the pan with 1 tablespoon butter. Cook for a few more minutes until nicely colored. Set aside and keep warm.

4 Heat the remaining oil in a medium saucepan and gently sauté the shallot for 5 minutes. Pour in the wine and stock, and bring to a gentle simmer.

5 Trim the brill fillets to neaten, and season them. Slip into the hot liquid. Poach the fish for 3–4 minutes until just tender. Do not overcook. Remove the fillets with a slotted spatula and keep them warm.

6 Strain the fish liquid through a fine sieve, then return to the pan. Boil rapidly until reduced by two-thirds, then stir in the remaining cream and some seasoning. Bring back to a gentle boil, then, on a low heat, whisk in the remaining butter, cut in small cubes, adding them one or two at a time. The sauce will thicken slightly and become glossy. Watch carefully to be sure that it doesn't "split."

7 Reheat the potato purée and divide among four warmed plates. Sit a brill fillet on top and arrange the glazed vegetables around. Spoon the *beurre rouge* over, sprinkle with the chopped parsley, and serve immediately.

Cod with Crisp Potatoes and Mustard Lentils

Fish, potatoes, and legumes are natural partners – think of fish and chips, which we Brits like with mushy peas. This is a more sophisticated variation, using the waxy red potatoes and dainty lentilles de Puy. A terrific light winter main course. **SERVES 4 AS A MAIN DISH**

1 pound even-sized red
  potatoes, scrubbed
¼ cup olive oil
4 fillets of cod, about 4 ounces each, with skin
½ cup *lentilles de Puy*
1 carrot
½ small onion
1 small stalk celery

1 tablespoon butter
1 shallot, minced
1 tablespoon capers, rinsed and patted dry
2 tablespoons Classic Vinaigrette (page 213)
  mixed with 1 teaspoon Dijon mustard
1 tablespoon chopped fresh chives
Sea salt and freshly ground black pepper

1 Cook the potatoes in boiling salted water for about 12 minutes until just tender. Drain and cool until you can handle them – they are best peeled hot (we put on rubber gloves). Cut into neat dice and toss with 1 tablespoon of the oil. Spread out on a tray, season, and let the potatoes absorb the oil as they cool.

2 Season the skin side of the cod with salt, rubbing it in nicely. Leave for half an hour. This helps to dry out the skin.

3 Place the lentils in a saucepan with the carrot, onion, and celery. Cover with cold water and bring to a boil. Simmer for about 15 minutes or until just cooked. Do not overcook or the lentils will break down. Drain immediately and discard the vegetables. Spread the lentils on a tray to cool. This stops them from cooking further.

4 When ready to cook, heat 1 tablespoon of the oil with the butter in a frying pan, and gently sauté the shallot for about 5 minutes. Scoop out the shallot and reserve. Add another tablespoon of oil to the pan, raise the heat, and tip in the diced potato. Cook until nicely golden brown, turning as necessary. Remove, mix with the shallot and capers, and keep warm.

5 Wipe out the pan and heat the remaining tablespoon of oil in it. When hot, add the fish, skin-side down. Cook until the skin crisps up nicely (make sure the heat isn't too high or the skin will burn). I always cook my cod for 90% of the total time on the skin side, then flip over just to brown the other side lightly. Cooking time depends on the thickness of the fillet, but is about 5 minutes in all. Check if the fish is cooked by pressing with the back of a fork. It should be lightly springy.

6 Reheat the lentils briefly in a saucepan, season, and stir in the vinaigrette and chives. Sit a cod fillet on each of four warmed plates, and spoon the lentils and the potatoes over. Serve hot.

Baby Red Mullets with Choucroute and Rhubarb

Here, little red mullets are filleted into a butterfly shape, then marinated and pan-fried. These are served on a salad that might make you gasp – choucroute with celery and rhubarb dressed with pink grapefruit vinaigrette. It has to be tried to be believed! Baby new potatoes and blanched spinach are good accompaniments. SERVES 4 AS A MAIN DISH

4 small red mullets, about 7 ounces each
  (or use pink or red bream)
3 tablespoons olive oil
2 pinches of saffron strands, crushed
4 stalks pink rhubarb, trimmed
4 inner stalks of celery, trimmed
½ cup *choucroute* (sauerkraut)
  from a jar, rinsed in cold water

⅔ cup Vegetable *Nage* (page 212)
1 tablespoon butter
1 pink grapefruit
5 tablespoons Classic Vinaigrette (page 213)
Leaves from 2 sprigs fresh cilantro, shredded
Sea salt and freshly ground black pepper

1 Cut the heads from the mullets, then, using kitchen scissors, cut along the belly of each fish and pull out the innards. Wash the cavity well under cold running water, rubbing away any blood spots. Lay the fish on a board and slit down to the tail end. Using the tip of a sharp filleting knife, loosen the backbone and finer bones from the flesh on both sides, then snip the bones carefully from the skin and discard. You want to fillet the fish, keeping the two sides joined together to form a butterfly shape. (See photographs of this technique on page 217.)

2 Pat the fish dry. Brush both sides with 1 tablespoon of the olive oil. Crush the saffron over the pink skins and rub in. Chill uncovered for 2 hours.

3 Meanwhile, make the *choucroute* salad. Cut the rhubarb and celery into thin *bâtons* 1½ inches long. Sweat the *choucroute* in the rest of the oil for 3 minutes, then add the rhubarb and celery. Cook for a further 2 minutes. Pour in the *nage* and seasoning. Dot with the butter and place a butter wrapper on top. Turn the heat right down and simmer very gently for 10 minutes, basting once or twice.

4 Meanwhile, peel the grapefruit, removing all white pith, and cut out the sections from the membrane. Break up the grapefruit sections in a bowl with a fork into little pink "tears." Mix with the vinaigrette.

5 Remove the *choucroute* from the heat and mix in half the grapefruit vinaigrette. Check the seasoning. Allow to cool to room temperature, then toss in the cilantro.

6 When ready to serve, heat a large non-stick frying pan and, when hot, fry the mullets for 3–4 minutes on the skin side until crisp. Flip them over carefully and cook briefly on the other side. Do not overcook, as the fish are small and delicate.

7 Divide the salad among four plates and place a pretty fish on top of each. Glaze with the rest of the grapefruit vinaigrette and serve.

Dorade Royale with a Ragoût of Blette

Dorades are confusing fish, or rather it is the variety of names attached to them that confuses. In French they are daurade, *and in English they're also known as breams. The dorade* royale *is the black bream – just one of the many varieties. Popular in many Mediterranean countries, dorades/breams are now being farmed, which makes them more available, although wild fish still has the edge on flavor and texture.* Blette *is the French name for Swiss chard. The stems and leaves are cooked separately, and then combined in a creamy grain mustard sauce.*

SERVES 4 AS A MAIN DISH

4 fillets of dorade *royale* (or other bream),
    about 4 ounces each, skin on
1 fat clove garlic, halved
3 tablespoons olive oil
1 pound Swiss chard
Juice of 1 lemon
2 tablespoons butter
$^1/_2$ cup Dark Chicken Stock (page 212)
$^1/_2$ cup heavy cream
1 tablespoon Pommery coarsegrain mustard
1 teaspoon fresh thyme leaves
Sea salt and freshly ground black pepper

1 Rub the fish flesh with the cut clove of garlic, then brush with half of the olive oil. Set aside to marinate in the fridge while you prepare the chard.
2 Wash the chard well and pat dry. Cut off the leaves and tear up into bite-size pieces. Using a swivel vegetable peeler, peel the stems lightly, then cut into 1$^1/_2$-inch-long *bâtons*. As you cut, drop them into cold water acidulated with the lemon juice, to prevent them from turning brown. When ready to cook, drain and pat dry.
3 Sweat the chard *bâtons* in the butter for 4–5 minutes, then add the stock and seasoning. Cook for another 4 minutes, then stir in the cream and mustard. Keep warm.
4 Meanwhile, blanch the chard leaves in a little boiling salted water for 2 minutes. Drain, refresh under cold running water, and drain well again. Stir into the creamy ragoût of chard *bâtons* and check the seasoning.
5 When ready to serve, heat a large non-stick pan and add a trickle of oil if you wish. Cook the fish fillets skin-side down for 3–4 minutes. Season the top as they cook, sprinkle with the thyme leaves, and baste once or twice with the pan juices. Turn the fillets carefully and cook the other side for a minute or until the fish feels just cooked. Do not overcook.
6 Spoon the ragoût into four shallow soup plates and sit a fish fillet on top of each. Serve hot.

A Quick Casserole of Squab

Casseroles don't have to be cooked long and slow. This one simmers diced winter vegetables in a rich red wine stock and is served with pan-fried breasts of squab. There's not much meat on a squab, so I only bother to cook the breasts, serving two for each portion.

SERVES 4 AS A MAIN DISH

4 nice fat squabs

About 5 ounces salsify

1 small head celeriac

1 small head rutabaga

2 medium parsnips

4 small red onions or 8 baby ones, peeled

¼ cup olive oil

1 sprig fresh rosemary

1 bay leaf

1¼ cups red wine

1 teaspoon tomato paste

1 teaspoon truffle oil

4 cups Dark Chicken Stock (page 212)

2 ounces baby button mushrooms

Sea salt and freshly ground black pepper

1 Cut the breasts from the squabs, so you have two breast halves per person. Discard the carcasses (or use to make stock). Set aside.

2 Peel the salsify, celeriac, rutabaga, and parsnips, and cut into large dice. If using small rather than baby onions, cut each in half. Heat 1½ tablespoons of the oil in a large pan and tip in all the vegetables including the onions. Toss in the herbs too. Sweat the vegetables for a good 10 minutes so they become nicely colored.

3 Meanwhile, boil the wine right down until reduced to around ½ cup. Stir the tomato paste and the truffle oil into the vegetables, then stir in the wine, stock, and some seasoning. Simmer uncovered until the vegetables are just tender, 10–12 minutes. The vegetables should have become wine-stained and the liquid reduced right down.

4 For the squabs, heat 1½ tablespoons of the remaining oil in a large frying pan. Season the breasts and quickly fry, skin-side down first, for a total of about 6 minutes. The breasts should be lightly springy when pressed and still a little pink inside.

5 Meanwhile, quickly sauté the mushrooms in the remaining 1 tablespoon of oil.

6 Divide all the vegetables among four warmed shallow soup plates. Set the squab breasts on top, season, and serve.

Duck Breasts with Endive Tarts

Gressingham ducks (a cross between the domestic duck and mallard) are one of my favorite things, full of flavor, with a skin that crisps nicely – as long as you score the skin closely and evenly. The endive tarts are an unusual accompaniment. They take a wee while to put together, but they are not difficult. You will need tartlet molds for this, about 4 inches in diameter and 1 inch deep. SERVES 4 AS A MAIN DISH

8 ounces puff pastry, preferably homemade (page 214)
4 medium heads Belgian endive
2½ tablespoons firmly packed light brown sugar
5 tablespoons butter
2 tablespoons balsamic vinegar
1 carrot, diced
¼ head celeriac, diced

½ small head Savoy cabbage, finely shredded
1 tablespoon olive oil
3 thick slices lean bacon, cut in small cubes
4 duck breasts, about 6 ounces each
1 tablespoon clear honey
2 whole cloves
Sea salt and freshly ground black pepper

1 Roll out the pastry to ¼-inch thickness. Cut out four disks at least 1¼ inches larger than the diameter of your tartlet molds. Prick the disks lightly and chill to rest. Preheat the oven to 400°.
2 Using a thin, sharp knife, tunnel-core the endive to remove as much of the hard core as possible, yet still keeping the leaves together. Cut the endive across so you have the dumpy section from each about 1¼ inches tall. Set aside. (Use the leafy tops in salads.)
3 In a small saucepan, dissolve the sugar in a small sprinkling of water, then add 4 tablespoons of the butter. Melt it, then boil for a minute or so. Mix in the vinegar. Pour this into the tartlet molds. Season the endive sections, then press one down into the caramel in each mold, cored-side up. (See photographs of this technique on page 218.)
4 Fit the pastry disks on top, tucking the edges down inside the mold around the sides. Bake for 12–15 minutes until the pastry is golden brown and crisp. Once or twice during baking, carefully tip out any juices from the molds. The endive will soften and take on a delicious caramelized flavor. Remove and allow to cool a bit while you make the rest of the dish.
5 Blanch the carrot and celeriac in boiling salted water for 3–4 minutes. Add the cabbage and cook for a further 2 minutes. Drain and refresh under cold running water. Wipe out the pan, heat the oil in it, and fry the bacon cubes for about 5 minutes, stirring once or twice. Set the pan aside.
6 Trim the duck breasts neatly, then score the skin very closely, taking care not to cut through the fat as well. The closer the scoring lines are together, the crisper the cooked skin will be. Heat a non-stick heavy-based frying pan and, when hot, put in the duck breasts, skin-side down. Cook for a few moments to brown. Fat will seep out. Tip this away so it does not burn. Turn the breasts over and brown the flesh side. Season as they cook. Turn over once more and baste the flesh side a few times with the pan juices. Cook for a total of 8–10 minutes. Duck is best served slightly pink and juicy.
7 Remove the duck breasts from the pan and keep warm, saving the juices that seep out. Drain off the excess fat from the pan, but hold back the meaty juices. Add the honey and cloves,

then return the duck breasts with their juices, and glaze with the honey mixture. Give the skin side one more turn in the pan to crisp it, then remove the breasts and leave to rest briefly.

8 Meanwhile, reheat the bacon, then add the butter and return the cabbage mixture to the pan. Stir gently until piping hot. Check the seasoning, then spoon in mounds in the center of four warmed plates. Sit the duck breasts on top (cut into slices diagonally, if you like) and trickle the pan juices over. Carefully unmold the endive tarts, loosening with a table knife if necessary, and place one on each plate. Using a thin spoon handle, gently separate the endive leaves to give a rose effect. Serve immediately.

Loin of Pork with Choucroute and Mustard-Cream Sauce

Pork is at its best in the middle of winter. Ask the butcher for a loin roast with the rind (skin) still on. This can be scored with deep cuts, so it will crisp to what we Brits call crackling – delicious with the pork. With this, I like to serve choucroute *cooked in the Alsace style with crisp bacon.*

SERVES 4 AS A MAIN DISH

1 boneless pork loin roast, about 2¼ pounds
1-pound jar *choucroute* (sauerkraut)
2 tablespoons olive oil
1 onion, sliced
3 thick slices lean bacon, cut in small cubes
3¼ cups Dark Chicken Stock (page 212)
⅔ cup heavy cream
1 tablespoon coarsegrain mustard
Sea salt and freshly ground black pepper

1 Preheat the oven to 400°. Heat a large frying pan on the stovetop until you can feel a strong heat rising. Put the pork roast in the pan, rind down, and press onto the hot pan (you might want to wrap your hand in a cloth to protect it). This will start the crackling crisping. Turn the roast and brown the rest of it.

2 Transfer the pork to a roasting pan, placing it rind side up, and sprinkle with sea salt. Roast for 30 minutes, then turn the temperature down to 350°. Roast for a further 30 minutes. Do not baste.

3 Meanwhile, rinse the *choucroute* in cold water and drain well. Heat 1 tablespoon of oil in a large saucepan and gently sauté the onion for 5 minutes until lightly colored. Stir in the bacon and continue cooking for about 3 minutes until crisp. Mix in the *choucroute*, and stir in 2 cups of the stock and freshly ground pepper. Bring to a boil, then cover and simmer very gently for about 20 minutes.

4 Meanwhile, boil the remaining stock until reduced by half. Tip out of the pan and save, and pour the cream into the pan. Bring the cream to a boil, slowly, then mix in the reduced stock plus the mustard. Check the seasoning and keep the sauce warm.

5 When the pork is nearing the end of its cooking, pierce the thickest section with a thin skewer. Clear juices should run out. If not, cook it for longer until the juices are clear. The pork should feel just firm when pressed, but not rock solid. Remove from the oven and allow to rest for about 10 minutes while you reheat the sauce and divide the *choucroute* among four warmed plates.

6 Carve the pork into fairly thick slices, and break up the crackling into pieces. Place on top of the *choucroute*, and spoon the sauce over. Sheer rustic pleasure.

Veal Chops with a Cream of Winter Vegetables

Veal is not overly popular, which is a shame because it has such a great flavor and is so versatile. You can serve it simply roasted or cooked with a sauce – a cream sauce as in a blanquette de veau *or a punchy tomato-based sauce such as in* osso bucco. *This is a nice recipe for a mid-week dinner – meat and vegetables all in one, celeriac and onions served with blanched baby spinach.*

SERVES 4 AS A MAIN DISH

4 veal loin chops, about 7 ounces each
¼ cup olive oil
1 teaspoon chopped fresh rosemary
8–12 baby onions
5 ounces celeriac
3 tablespoons butter
7 ounces baby leaf spinach (about 2 cups)
1 tablespoon Dijon mustard
1 cup heavy cream
Sea salt and freshly ground black pepper

1 Trim the chops, then place flat on a board. Using a rolling pin, beat the loin lightly to flatten slightly. Brush both sides of each chop with a little olive oil and sprinkle with rosemary. Leave to marinate for about 2 hours.

2 Meanwhile, blanch the onions in boiling water for 30 seconds. Drain and rinse in cold water. The skins should slip off easily. Heat 1 tablespoon of oil in a small pan and sauté the onions for 5–7 minutes until golden brown. Remove with a slotted spoon and set aside.

3 Peel the celeriac and cut into dice (you should have about 1 cup). Heat the remaining oil and 2 tablespoons of the butter in the same pan and sauté the celeriac for about 5 minutes, turning once or twice. Season nicely and return the onions to the pan. Set aside.

4 Blanch the spinach in boiling water for 1 minute, then drain and refresh under cold running water. Drain well again and press out as much water as possible. (In my kitchen, I squeeze the leaves in a clean dish towel.)

5 Stir the mustard and cream into the celeriac and onions, and bring slowly to a boil. Check the seasoning. Keep warm.

6 Now for the veal. Heat a heavy-based non-stick frying pan and, when hot, put in the veal chops. Season as they cook, allowing 3–4 minutes on each side. Baste once or twice with any pan juices or any leftover marinade.

7 Reheat the spinach with the remaining butter. Divide the celeriac and onions among four warmed plates, sit the chops on top, and spoon the spinach around. Serve hot.

Veal Cutlets with Fondant Kohlrabi and Baby Globe Artichokes

Winter is a good season for using baby globe artichokes. These are so young the chokes have not yet formed, so can be cooked and eaten whole. Winter is also the time for kohlrabi, with its intriguing turnip-like flavor. If you take time to prepare special vegetable dishes, then it makes sense to serve with a quick-cook cut of meat. My favorite is a slice of veal from the round, which is called a cutlet or escalope. **SERVES 4 AS A MAIN DISH**

4 baby globe artichokes
Juice of ½ lemon
1 medium head kohlrabi, about 1 pound
2 tablespoons butter
1 tablespoon olive oil
⅔ cup Light Chicken Stock (page 212)
4 veal cutlets, about 4 ounces each
3 tablespoons all-purpose flour
3 tablespoons clarified butter
2 teaspoons chopped fresh chervil
2 teaspoons chopped fresh parsley
2 teaspoons chopped fresh chives
Sea salt and freshly ground black pepper

1 First prepare the artichokes. Trim the tips of the leaves and snap off the stems. Drop into a pan of boiling water with half the lemon juice. Cook for 5 minutes, then drain upside down in a colander. Cool.

2 Peel the kohlrabi and slice into ½-inch-thick rounds. Heat half the butter and the oil in a *sauteuse* or shallow saucepan. Fry the kohlrabi slices quickly on both sides to brown nicely, then season and pour in the stock. Add half of the remaining butter to the pan and cover with a butter wrapper. Simmer gently until the stock has evaporated and the slices have softened, 10–12 minutes. Do not turn them. Leave in the pan, but remove from the heat.

3 Now for the veal. Place one of the cutlets between sheets of parchment paper and beat lightly with the flat of a metal cleaver or rolling pin. Don't whack the life out of the meat – just a light battening to flatten and tenderize. Repeat with the other cutlets. Season the flour and toss the veal in it, shaking off any excess.

4 Heat the clarified butter in a heavy-based non-stick frying pan and lay in the veal. Fry quickly for a minute to sear, then slip in the remaining bit of butter. When it froths, turn the veal over. Baste with the frothing butter and cook for 1–2 minutes until the meat feels just firm. Don't overcook. Toss in the chopped herbs, season lightly, and squeeze the remaining lemon juice over.

5 Serve the veal on warmed plates. Reheat the artichokes (in a little buttery water) and the kohlrabi, spoon onto the plates with the veal, and serve.

My Special Steak Tartare and Fries

There is an art to making a steak tartare. It is one of the great skills of l'art de la table, *as practiced by top front-of-house staff. My maître d', Jean-Claude Breton, is truly a master of this art! He will tell you that the main requirement is the very best tenderloin steak from the very best beef, which can only be from well-hung Aberdeen Angus cattle. The next secret of success is to chop the meat by hand, using two razor-sharp, heavy-duty cook's knives. Often a good butcher will arrange to have your knives sharpened for you – just check what day his knife grinder calls. Finally, for the fries you also need good ingredients. We like to fry the potatoes in light olive oil, but peanut oil is also good, as it can be taken to a high temperature and has a fairly neutral flavor, ideal for deep frying. Note that this recipe contains raw beef and raw egg yolk.*

SERVES 2 AS A MAIN DISH

8 ounces best lean beef tenderloin

2 teaspoons minced capers

2 teaspoons minced gherkins

2 teaspoons minced red onion

2 teaspoons minced fresh parsley

2 teaspoons tomato ketchup

2 teaspoons Dijon mustard

½–1 teaspoon crushed sea salt

A few dashes each of hot pepper
  and Worcestershire sauces

1 extra large egg yolk
  (ideally organic)

Fries

1 pound medium boiling potatoes, peeled

Light olive oil or peanut oil for deep frying

Sea salt for sprinkling

1 It is important that everything is kept chilled when making this recipe – the chopping board and mixing bowl especially. Don't overwork the beef, so the texture remains fresh. Cut the beef into thin slices, then cut the slices into very thin strips. Gather a few strips together and cut across in very tiny cubes. (See photographs of this technique on page 220.)

2 Place the beef in the chilled bowl, spreading the meat up the sides of the bowl to chill further. Add all the remaining ingredients and mix quickly together with a fork until well blended. Shape into two patties and place on chilled plates. Cover and set these in the fridge to keep cool while you make the fries.

3 Cut the potatoes into ½-inch-thick sticks. Don't rinse them – simply lay out on a cloth, season with salt, and leave to "dégorge" for 5 minutes, to dry out a little. Pat dry.

4 Heat a 2-inch depth of oil in a deep frying pan to 350°. Slip the potato sticks into the hot oil (ideally in a frying basket) and fry for 3 minutes or so until softened but not browned. Remove from the oil, and reheat it again to 350°. Return the potatoes and fry until golden brown and crisp. Drain on paper towels and sprinkle with salt.

5 Serve the fries in a bowl with the steak tartare.

Braised Oxtail with Parsnip Purée

Braised oxtail is one of the great British classic dishes, with rich, velvety meat that softens in long, slow cooking. The slices step down in size as the tail narrows. Ideally, you need two good slices per portion. You may find it wise to buy two oxtails and have some leftover for the next day, or to freeze. A comforting parsnip mash is great for soaking up the rich gravy-sauce. This one is a reminder of my first restaurant, the Aubergine. Parsnip purée was so popular, I had to keep it on the menu until I got tired of cooking it. Now I can reintroduce it. Both elements of this dish can be cooked a day ahead and reheated to serve – another plus in its favor.

SERVES 4 AS A MAIN DISH

2 oxtails, about 2¼ pounds each,
  cut in 1¼-inch slices
1¾ cups red wine
1 sprig fresh thyme
1 bay leaf
¼ cup olive oil
2 carrots, chopped
1 red onion, chopped
4 cups Dark Chicken Stock (page 212)
Sea salt and freshly ground black pepper

Parsnip purée
4 medium, chunky parsnips
2 tablespoons butter
1 tablespoon olive oil
1 medium potato, peeled and roughly chopped
1¼ cups Light Chicken Stock (page 212)
⅔ cup heavy cream

1 Marinate the oxtails in the wine. The easiest way to do this is to put the oxtail into a large plastic bag and pour in the wine and herbs. Seal the bag and rub all together. Store in the fridge overnight.

2 When ready to cook, remove the oxtails and reserve the wine. Heat 2 tablespoons of the olive oil in a large cast-iron casserole and brown the oxtail pieces in succession. Drain on paper towels.

3 Heat the remaining oil in the pan and sauté the carrots and onion for about 5 minutes until softened. Add the wine marinade (with herbs) and cook until reduced by two-thirds. Pour in the stock and bring to a boil. Return the oxtail pieces and season nicely, then cover and simmer on the gentlest of heats for almost 3 hours until the meat is very tender and falls from the bone when prodded.

4 Meanwhile, make the parsnip purée. Peel the parsnips and cut in thick chunks from around the core. Discard the core. Chop the parsnips roughly. Heat the butter and olive oil in a shallow saucepan and gently sauté the parsnips and potato until pale golden brown. Pour in the stock, season, and bring to a boil. Cover with one or two butter wrappers and simmer for about 15 minutes until the vegetables are soft and the liquid has evaporated.

5 Pour in the cream, bring back to a boil, and simmer for a few minutes until almost all has gone. Scoop into a food processor and blend until velvety and smooth. Check the seasoning.

6 Spoon the oxtails onto warmed serving plates or a large serving platter. Strain the cooking liquid, reheat, and spoon over the oxtail. To garnish, I suggest diagonal slices of carrots cooked with a little butter, water, and crushed garlic. Really nice. Serve with the parsnip purée.

Crispy Pig's Feet

This recipe is a labor of love, but if you have ever eaten stuffed pig's feet (which we Brits call trotters) and love cooking, then you'll want to try making them. Pig's feet generally have to be ordered ahead – make sure you get them with a long length of bone, about 6 inches, above the actual hoof. You can order the ham hocks at the same time. A razor-sharp, thin-bladed knife is essential, because you need to skin the feet cleanly. I like to serve this with fried quail eggs and wafer-thin slices of fresh truffle on top – very posh bacon and eggs. SERVES **4** AS A MAIN DISH

2 ham hocks, to give you about
  1 pound meat after cooking
4 long-length pig's feet (see above),
  singed of hairs
1 onion, half sliced and half diced
2 carrots, diced
1 stalk celery, diced
1 fresh bouquet garni (a bay leaf, sprig
  fresh thyme, crushed parsley stems,
  and celery leaf tied together)
4–5 tablespoons olive oil
4 fat cloves garlic, chopped
1 bay leaf
1 sprig fresh thyme

4 teaspoons tomato paste
1 bottle red wine
4 cups Dark Chicken Stock (page 212)
1 pair sweetbreads, prepared and cooked
  (see Sweetbreads with Shallot and
  Mushroom Marmalade, page 147),
  then cut in 6–8 pieces (optional)
Sea salt and freshly ground black pepper

To serve (optional)
Mixed salad leaves
Classic Vinaigrette (page 213)

1 Start the preparation 24 hours ahead. First, put the ham hocks in separate bowls of cold water and set aside to soak. Then skin the pig's feet: Using a very sharp, thin-bladed boning knife, score right down the thick skin of one foot to the top of the first knuckle. Working the knife tip under the skin, start to shave away the skin from the bone. Try to ensure you don't take any fat or veins with the skin. Keep shaving and pulling the skin away until you get right down to the first knuckle.

2 Hold the foot in a clean cloth and let the skin fall over your hand. Score around the partly exposed knuckle and pull the skin away. You should now be able to cut away the long bone, leaving you with a large, loose flap of skin and the end of the knuckle with the toes still attached. It should look like an empty glove puppet at this point. One final tip is to try not to nick the skin as you work it from the bone – I know it might be difficult, but it will stop the filling from spilling out later on.

3 Skin the other feet the same way. To encourage you in this labor of love, let me tell you that my young chefs can skin a pig's foot in 12 seconds, or so they claim. I've never timed them, but they do work fast and clean.

4 Put the skins in a bowl of cold water and soak for 24 hours to remove any vestiges of blood. Drain and pat dry with paper towels.

5 When ready to cook, drain the ham hocks and put them in a pan of fresh water to cover. Add the sliced onion, half the carrots and celery, the bouquet garni, and pepper. Bring to a boil,

200 winter

skimming off any scum, then reduce the heat and simmer very gently for about 2 hours until the liquid reduces right down.

6 Allow to cool, then strain the ham stock. Shred the meat from the bone and set aside. Discard the vegetables and bouquet garni. Boil the ham stock down until reduced by half, then set aside. It should set to a jelly as it cools.

7 Sauté the rest of the onion, carrot, and celery in 2 tablespoons of the oil for 5–10 minutes until softened and caramelized. Add the garlic, bay leaf, thyme, and tomato paste and cook for 2 minutes, then pour in all the wine. Cook right down until reduced by three-fourths.

8 Pour in the chicken stock and add the pig's feet skins. Bring to a boil, then partially cover and simmer very gently for 3½–4 hours. Do not stir if you can help it, as you might cut the skin by mistake. The skin is ready when you can press a piece on the side of the pan with your two fingers and pierce it easily. Cool for 10 minutes in the cooking liquid, then carefully remove to a wire rack and cool further. Discard the liquid.

9 Now you can cut off the toes. You should have four large pieces of very soft, deep red skin. Pat them dry. Line a chopping board with a large sheet of plastic wrap. Lay a skin along the length, and fix another skin butting up to the first and slightly overlapping it. Repeat with the other two skins, to make a rectangle of skin about 6 by 15 inches. Brush generously with the partially set ham stock. This helps to hold it all together. (In the restaurant kitchen we spread a thin layer of chicken *mousseline* on the skin, but ham stock will do almost as well.)

10 Lay the shredded ham down the center, mounding it up neatly. If using the sweetbreads, put half the ham on the skins, arrange the sweetbreads on top, nicely spaced out, and cover with the rest of the ham.

11 Fold one side of the skin over the filling firmly and neatly, and roll evenly into a "sausage." Wrap well in foil, making sure there are no gaps or bubbles, and twist the ends tightly. Chill for 12 hours at least.

12 When you are ready to serve, use a very sharp or serrated knife, dipped in hot water, to slice the roll into 12 medallions. Heat the last of the oil in a frying pan and quickly fry the medallions for about 3 minutes on each side until crisp. Serve on a well-dressed mixed salad.

Orange and Lemon Tart

I blush to say I am frequently complimented on the orange and lemon tart we serve at the restaurant – I must share the credit with my pâtisserie chefs, led by Thierry Besselieur. The perfect French lemon tart really depends on the skill of the cook, rolling out the rich sweet pastry until very thin without it breaking, boiling the fruit juices to concentrate the flavor, and then baking the filling at a very low temperature until it is just softly set. As a final flourish, we add the thinnest crisp sugar crust, made not just with one caramelized sugar dusting, but two. Try it.
SERVES 4–6

1 quantity rich sweet pastry (see Pear and Frangipane Tart, page 153)
2 tablespoons confectioners' sugar
Confit of Orange and Lemon (page 215), optional

Filling
2$\frac{1}{2}$ cups orange juice
Juice of 2 lemons
Grated zest of 1 lemon
Grated zest of 1 orange
1 cup granulated sugar
6 egg yolks, beaten
$\frac{2}{3}$ cup heavy cream

1 Roll out the pastry dough as thinly as you are able, to a round about 12 inches in diameter, large enough to line an 8-inch tart pan, 1–1$\frac{1}{4}$ inches deep, comfortably with overhang. You could do this on a lightly floured board, or between two lightly floured sheets of plastic wrap. Lift the dough on the rolling pin into the tart pan (or a flan ring set on a heavy, flat baking sheet). Press the dough well onto the bottom and sides of the pan and pinch together or patch any gaps with dough trimmings. There should be a fair amount of overhang (don't trim it off). Place the pan on a baking sheet.

2 Fit a large sheet of foil into the pastry shell, bringing it well up the sides. Fill with baking beans. Chill for 20 minutes, while you preheat the oven to 350°.

3 Bake the pastry shell for 12–15 minutes until just set. Remove the foil and beans. Return the pastry shell to the oven to bake for 5 more minutes. Trim the top of the pastry shell level with the pan using a very sharp knife, then set aside to cool while you make the filling.

4 Reduce the oven temperature to its lowest setting, which will probably be about 250°. Allow about 20 minutes for the temperature to fall.

5 For the filling, boil the orange and lemon juices together until reduced to about $\frac{3}{4}$ cup. Cool. Beat the lemon and orange zest with the granulated sugar and egg yolks. Add the cream and then the cooled juice.

6 Place the pastry shell on the pulled-out oven shelf and slowly pour in the filling, taking it up to as near the rim of the shell as possible. Very, very carefully push the tart back into the oven and bake for about 35 minutes. The filling should still be quite soft. Turn off the oven and leave the

tart to cool inside until it sets enough so that it can be removed without spilling. Cool completely until lightly set, then chill.

7 Sift half of the confectioners' sugar over the top of the tart in an even layer. Immediately caramelize the sugar with a blowtorch. Let this cool and crisp, then sift another layer of confectioners' sugar on top and caramelize that. Leave to cool completely.

8 Cut the tart into portions using a long, sharp knife and serve with a trickle of cream, if you like. We also add a decoration of *confit* of orange and lemon slices. Should the mood arise, then do try to make them, as they are a nice complement to the tart.

Apple, Prune, and Butterscotch Compote

My desserts are always served in diminutive portions. I reckon after four or five courses, my guests want just a taste or two of an intensely flavored dessert. This is such a sweet – delicious Armagnac-soaked Agen prunes served in small shot glasses topped with an apple and butterscotch purée and thick creamy yogurt. The yogurt can be strained overnight to make it even more luscious. If you wish to serve larger portions, then spoon into small wine glasses.

SERVES 4–8, DEPENDING ON SERVING SIZE

¹/₂ cup Armagnac, Calvados, or other brandy

8–10 plump semi-dried (*mi-cuit*) Agen prunes

1 large Granny Smith apple, peeled, cored, and chopped

1 vanilla bean

¹/₂ cup + 2 tablespoons sugar

7 tablespoons unsalted butter

¹/₂ cup heavy cream

About 1¹/₄ cups thick Greek-style whole-milk yogurt

1 Heat the brandy of your choice in a small saucepan, without letting it boil. Remove from the heat and stir in the prunes. Leave to macerate overnight.

2 The next day, drain the prunes, remove the pits, and chop the flesh roughly. Set aside.

3 Put the chopped apple in another small pan and trickle over 2 tablespoons of water. Slit the vanilla bean and, using the tip of the knife, scrape out the seeds. Mix with 2 tablespoons of the sugar, add to the pan, and stir into the apple. Heat until sizzling, then cover and cook for 5–7 minutes, stirring occasionally, until soft and pulpy. Cool, then crush to a chunky purée with a fork.

4 In another saucepan, gently heat the remaining sugar with a splash of water until melted, stirring occasionally. When clear, raise the heat, stir in the butter, and cook to a light caramel color. Do not stir or you will make fudge.

5 Remove from the heat and cool for 5 minutes, then mix in the cream. Cool to room temperature, then mix in the apple and chill.

6 Divide the prunes among the glasses of your choice. Stir the yogurt until smooth, then spoon half on top, followed by the apple mixture. Finally, finish with the rest of the yogurt.

Note: I also add tiny sprigs of sugared fresh cilantro leaf to decorate. Make these by dipping sprigs of cilantro into beaten egg white and then sugar, and leaving to dry on parchment paper.

Praline Soufflés

Don't think you cannot possibly make a hot sweet soufflé for dessert. We make dozens a day, and all arrive at the table as towering triumphs. It is true that you will have to disappear into the kitchen to beat the egg whites and fold them into the base mixture. And yes, you will have to wait 15 minutes for the soufflés to cook, but at a private party most people expect to have a good pause after the main course, to truly appreciate the trouble you have gone to for the dessert. Also, it's a good excuse for another glass of wine. SERVES **6**

1 cup whole milk
½ cup superfine sugar
½ quantity Praline (page 215)
¼ cup all-purpose flour
4 extra large eggs, 2 of them separated
A little melted butter, for the ramekins
Confectioners' sugar for dusting (optional)

1 First make the base mix. Heat the milk with half of the superfine sugar and all but ¼ cup of the praline in a heavy-based saucepan.

2 Meanwhile, beat together the flour, 2 whole eggs, and 2 yolks in a large bowl. Place the bowl on a damp cloth to hold it steady, and gradually whisk in the hot praline milk. Beat well, then return to the pan and cook on a gentle simmer until very thick and smooth. Remove and cool.

3 Have ready the 2 egg whites and remaining superfine sugar. Brush the inside of six ramekins (about 3½ inches in diameter) with melted butter and dust with the reserved praline, shaking out any excess. Place on a baking sheet. Preheat the oven to 375°.

4 When ready to cook, beat the egg whites until thick and glossy and holding soft peaks. Gradually beat in the sugar. Fold the meringue (as it is now) into the base mix. Spoon this into the ramekins right up to the rim, and spread the tops level with a metal spatula.

5 Bake for 15 minutes until risen and firm. If you have time, sift some confectioners' sugar on the tops, although you may prefer to walk quickly to the table with the soufflés.

Note: Here's a useful tip. Instead of decanting the baked soufflés onto a tray, take the baking sheet straight to the table and scoop off the ramekins with a slotted spatula onto waiting dessert plates.

My Plum Tarts

This takes me back to my days as a catering student. The idea is based on tarte Tatin, *but uses sliced red plums. The ingredients are simple, but the method needs to be followed carefully. You need tartlet molds (without loose bases) about 4 inches in diameter.*

SERVES 4

1 quantity rich sweet pastry (see Pear and Frangipane Tart, page 153)
12 large red plums
4 tablespoons unsalted butter
½ cup sugar
4 whole cloves

1 Roll out the pastry dough to ¼-inch thickness. Cut out four 5-inch rounds, re-rolling if necessary. Prick the centers of the rounds lightly and set aside.

2 Cut the plums in half, remove the pits, and slice each half into four. Divide the butter among four tartlet molds and smear over the bottom. Sprinkle 1½ tablespoons of sugar into each mold. Preheat the oven to 375°.

3 Press the plum slices into the butter and sugar, and press a clove in the center of the fruit in each mold. Set the molds in a large frying pan and place over a steady heat.

4 The butter and sugar will start to melt and caramelize in the heat. Tilt and roll the frying pan over the heat to shake the molds a bit and even out the browning. After a few minutes you may notice some juice seeping out from the plums. Wrap your fingers in a cloth, then lift up each mold and tip the juice out. This helps to keep the plums dry and caramelize them even more. When the plums look lightly caramelized, remove from the heat and cool slightly.

5 Set a pastry round over each mold and tuck the edges down inside the rim. Prick the tops once or twice, and bake for 12–15 minutes until the pastry is golden brown and crisp. Remove and cool.

6 To serve, upturn a dessert plate over each tart mold and carefully turn over. Serve with cream, mascarpone, or crème fraîche.

Winter Fruits in Malibu Syrup with Mascarpone Quenelles

This is a quick hot dessert – sliced winter fruits steeped in a hot syrup laced with Malibu, a rum-flavored crème liqueur. As a flavor variation, when making the syrup, I caramelize the sugar first until light golden brown, then add the water and simmer for a minute or two. Serve the fruits in shallow fruit dishes and top with quenelles of whipped cream and mascarpone, which melt as you serve. **SERVES 4–6**

¹/₂ cup granulated sugar

1 strip lemon zest

2 tablespoons Malibu or white rum

About ¹/₂ cup fresh cranberries

1 quince

1 large pear

1 large, crisp apple

4 red plums, pitted

1 just ripe banana

¹/₃ cup confectioners' sugar, sifted

Coconut Tuiles (page 215) or shortbreads
  (see Roasted Figs with Cinnamon
  Shortbreads, page 91) for serving

Quenelles

²/₃ cup heavy cream

2 teaspoons sugar

1 vanilla bean

3 tablespoons mascarpone, softened

1 Melt the granulated sugar with a splash of water in a heavy-based saucepan, stirring once or twice. Raise the heat and, without stirring, cook to a light golden caramel.

2 Remove and plunge the base of the pan into a bowl of ice water to stop the browning. Cool until warm, then stir in 1 cup water and the lemon zest. Return to the heat and stir until you have a golden syrup. Boil for a minute or so, then add the Malibu and cranberries, and stir. Set aside.

3 Peel and core the quince and pear. Core the apple, but leave the skin on. Slice these fruits thinly along with the plums and banana. Put all the fruits in a bowl.

4 Heat a large non-stick frying pan until very hot. Sprinkle the confectioners' sugar over the fruits and toss to coat, then immediately tip them all into the dry hot pan. Shake the pan well and carefully turn the fruits, which by now should be caramelizing nicely. Cook for a minute or so, then add to the cranberry and Malibu syrup and mix gently. Cool until just warm. Remove the lemon zest strip.

5 For the quenelles, whip the cream with the sugar until softly stiff. Slit the vanilla bean and scrape out the seeds with a knife tip. Mix the seeds into the cream along with the softened mascarpone. Chill lightly.

6 When ready to serve, divide the fruits among sundae dishes or shallow bowls. Using two soup spoons dipped in hot water, shape the cream into 4–6 quenelles and place on top of the fruits. Serve with coconut tuiles or shortbreads.

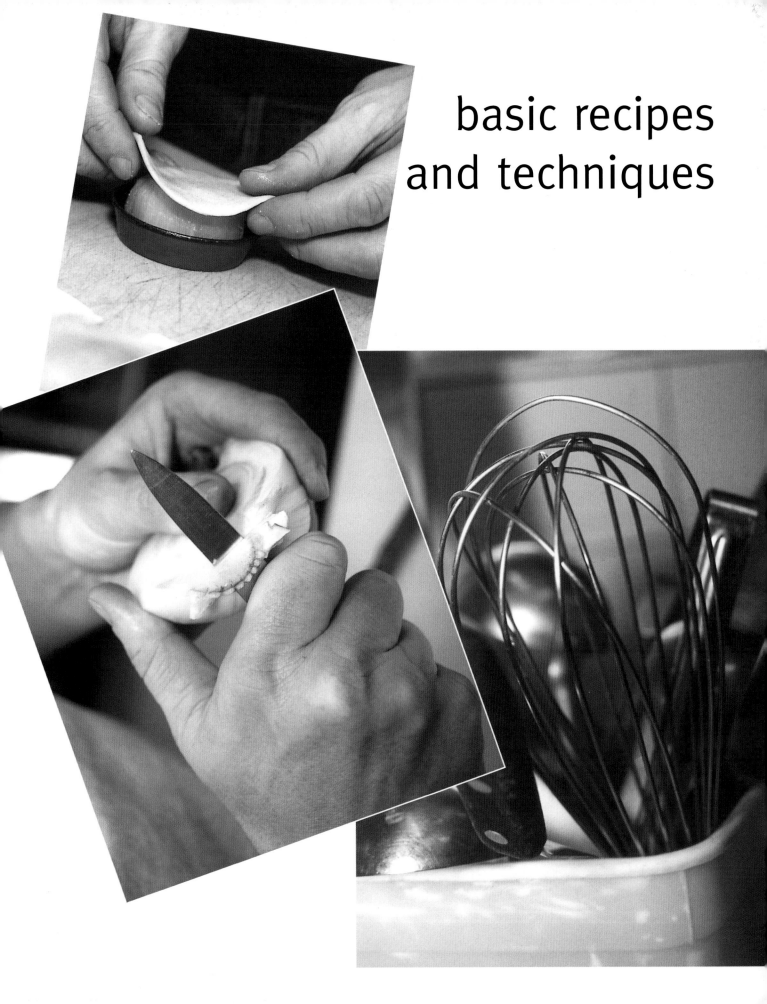

basic recipes and techniques

Several of my recipes require standard preparations, which in a restaurant kitchen we always have on hand. For those that can be kept, I suggest you make up good-size batches and either store in the fridge or freezer. The stocks are most useful frozen in 1-cup and 2-cup blocks. (Do label them before freezing – they can all look the same once frozen!)

The stocks are best strained through cheesecloth, which can be easily bought from good kitchenware stores. It is very cheap and can be washed in the machine time and time again.

Light chicken stock

Place $6^{1}/_{2}$–7 pounds raw chicken carcasses or bony portions in a large stockpot. Add 5 quarts of cold water, 3 quartered onions, 2 chopped leeks, 2 large chopped carrots, 4 chopped celery stalks, 1 small head garlic (cut across in half), 1 large sprig fresh thyme, and 1 tablespoon sea salt. Bring slowly to a boil, skimming off any scum that rises using a large metal spoon (not slotted because the scum can drain through). Boil for 5 minutes, then turn the heat right down and simmer for 3–4 hours. Cool and allow the solids to settle. Line a colander with a sheet of wet cheesecloth and slowly pour the stock through. Cool and chill. This can be kept in the fridge for up to 3 days or frozen. It makes about 3 quarts of lovely stock.

For **dark chicken stock,** first roast the chicken carcasses in a preheated 400° oven for about 20 minutes, turning frequently. Drain off the fat and proceed as above.

Vegetable *nage*

One of the most useful stocks to have on hand, this is made slightly differently from other stocks.

Put the following ingredients into a large stockpot: 3 chopped onions, 6 chopped carrots, 2 chopped celery stalks, 1 chopped leek, 1 small head garlic (split across in two), 1 quartered lemon, $^{1}/_{4}$ teaspoon each white and pink peppercorns, 1 small bay leaf, and 4 star anise. Pour in 2 quarts of cold water, bring slowly to a boil, and simmer for 10 minutes. Remove from the heat and mix in 1 cup dry white wine. Add a sprig each fresh tarragon,

basil, cilantro, thyme, and curly-leaf parsley. Cool, then decant into a large bowl and store in the fridge for about 24 hours. Strain through a cheesecloth-lined colander. This can be kept in the fridge for up to 4 days or frozen. Makes about $1^{1}/_{2}$ quarts.

Fish stock

White fish bones are the most useful, e.g. those from turbot, sole, haddock, hake, and so on, not oily fish such as salmon. You'll need about $3^{1}/_{2}$–$4^{1}/_{2}$ pounds of bones. If using fish heads too, cut out the eyes and the gills.

Gently sweat 1 small chopped onion, 1 chopped leek, 1 chopped celery stalk, 1 small chopped bulb fennel, and 2 whole garlic cloves in a little olive oil for 10 minutes. Add the fish bones (and heads) and $1^{1}/_{4}$ cups dry white wine, and cook until the wine evaporates. Cover with about 3 quarts of cold water, and add a fresh bouquet garni (bay leaf, sprig fresh thyme, and some parsley stems tied together), 1 small sliced lemon, and a few white peppercorns. Bring to a boil, skimming well, then simmer for 20 minutes only – no longer or the stock will become bitter. Cool so the solids settle, then strain through a cheesecloth-lined colander. This can be kept for up to 3 days in the fridge or frozen. Makes $2^{1}/_{2}$ quarts.

Court bouillon

Use this for poaching lobsters and whole fish. It can be used up to three times, straining in between.

Simply put all of the following ingredients into a large stockpot: 2 chopped leeks, 3 chopped carrots, 3 chopped onions, 2 chopped celery stalks, 2 chopped bulbs fennel, and 4 large garlic cloves (unpeeled). Cover with about 3 quarts of cold water and add 1 large sprig each fresh thyme, parsley, basil, and tarragon, plus 1 tablespoon sea salt, 2 sliced lemons, 4 star anise, and $1\frac{1}{4}$ cups dry white wine. Bring to a boil, then simmer gently for 30 minutes. Strain through a cheesecloth-lined colander. This can be kept for up to 5 days in the fridge or frozen. Makes about $1\frac{1}{2}$ quarts.

Classic vinaigrette

This has many uses apart from dressing salads.

Whisk together 1 cup extra virgin olive oil and 1 cup peanut oil with 1 teaspoon fine sea salt, $\frac{1}{4}$ teaspoon ground black pepper, the juice of 1 lemon, $\frac{1}{4}$ cup white wine vinegar, and $\frac{1}{4}$ cup sherry vinegar. Store in a large screwtop jar and shake to re-emulsify before use. Makes about $2\frac{1}{2}$ cups.

Mayonnaise

Whisk 2 egg yolks, 1 teaspoon white wine vinegar, 1 teaspoon English mustard powder, and a little seasoning together in a bowl. (Sit the bowl on a damp cloth to hold it steady.) Using $1\frac{1}{4}$ cups peanut oil or half peanut and half light olive oil, drop in a trickle from a teaspoon and beat hard until mixed. Repeat again and again, gradually adding a tad more oil each time, but always make sure the previous amount is well mixed in before adding more. Gradually increase the amount of oil added as the mixture gets thicker and more creamy. When all the oil is mixed in, whisk in 2 tablespoons cold water.

Check the seasoning. This can be kept, stored in a sealed container, for up to a week in the fridge. Makes $1\frac{1}{2}$ cups.

Peach chutney

If you can, use white-fleshed peaches for this chutney. Failing that, yellow peaches will suffice. Buy half of the fruits slightly underripe and a little firm, and the rest slightly overripe and full of flavor. The chutney is also good made with pears, apricots, and even mango.

Wash and pit $2\frac{1}{4}$ pounds fresh peaches, then chop into small bite-size pieces. (If using a mixture of slightly underripe peaches and fully ripe ones, set the fully ripe ones aside to add later.) Put the peaches into a large saucepan or preserving kettle and add 1 apple (peeled, cored, and minced), 8 ounces tomatoes (skinned and chopped), 1 minced medium onion, 2 crushed fat cloves garlic, 2 tablespoons grated fresh ginger root, the grated zest and juice of 2 limes, $1\frac{1}{2}$ cups sugar, 1 tablespoon sea salt, 1 teaspoon ground cinnamon, $1\frac{1}{2}$ teaspoons freshly grated nutmeg, $1\frac{1}{2}$ teaspoons ground white pepper, $1\frac{1}{4}$ cups white wine vinegar, and $1\frac{1}{3}$ cups sliced almonds. Bring slowly to a boil, stirring until all the sugar has dissolved. Simmer, uncovered, for about 15 minutes, stirring once or twice. Add the ripe peaches (if using), return to a simmer, and continue cooking for a further 10 minutes. The mixture should be nice and syrupy, with the underripe peaches still holding a little texture.

While the chutney is bubbling merrily, wash two canning jars (about 1-pint size) and sterilize in

boiling water (the lids too). Ladle the chutney into the hot, dry jars, and cover. For safety, process in a boiling-water bath. Leave until cold, then label and store. The chutney will keep well, unopened, for a good few months, but once opened, store it in the fridge. Makes about 2 pints.

Confit of cèpes

Wash 1 pound fresh cèpes and dry well with paper towels. Remove the stems and dice. Dice the caps too. Heat 2 tablespoons olive oil in a large frying pan and quickly sauté the cèpes until lightly browned. Remove from the heat. Heat 1 cup goose fat to the lowest temperature your stovetop can go, preferably below 212°. Add 1 sprig fresh thyme and stir in the cèpes. Cook very gently for about 15 minutes, then cool in the fat. Transfer to a clean jar and store in the fridge until required.

Pickled chanterelles

You can store these in a jar in the fridge and use them in many different ways, just as you would capers or chunky relishes.

Trim the bases of about 10 ounces small winter chanterelles. Wash to remove any dirt, then pat dry with paper towels. Make up $1\frac{1}{4}$ cups Classic Vinaigrette (see left) and bring to a boil in a saucepan. When boiling, stir in the chanterelles. Return to a boil, then remove from the heat and leave to steep until cool. Store in a glass container in the fridge and use within 10 days.

Stock syrup

I flavor my stock syrups in various ways – you may find a strip or two of lemon zest is best for general uses, but other ingredients could include a split stem of lemongrass, a cinnamon stick, or even a couple of star anise.

Slowly dissolve 1¼ cups sugar in 2 cups water. When clear, add the flavoring and simmer for 5 minutes, then cool. The stock syrup will keep for a month in the fridge; thereafter it benefits from re-boiling. Makes about 3 cups.

Puff pastry

Bought puff pastry may be convenient and good at rising evenly, but nothing beats homemade for buttery flavor and melt-in-the-mouth texture. Make this in a large batch and freeze in easy-to-use, individually wrapped blocks.

Sift ¼ teaspoon salt with 3⅓ cups all-purpose flour, and divide off ⅓ cup. Divide off 4 tablespoons butter from 1 pound (4 sticks). Cut the remaining butter into small dice and mix with the ⅓ cup flour (do this in a food processor if possible). Spoon onto a large sheet of plastic wrap and shape into a large rectangle about 6 by 8 inches. Try to keep the edges neat, as it helps later on. Set aside.

Rub the 4 tablespoons butter into the 3 cups of flour. (This is best done in a food processor.) Trickle in 1 teaspoon of fresh lemon juice and enough ice water so the mixture just comes together in a mass – this may take up to 1¼ cups of water, added gradually. Knead lightly to a smooth dough.

Roll out on a lightly floured board to a rectangle about 10 by 14 inches, keeping the edges neat and straight with even corners. Place the butter rectangle on one side and fold over the other half of the dough to enclose it. Press the edges to seal.

Carefully roll out the dough until it is about three times as long as it is wide. Make sure the butter doesn't break through. Now, fold the top third down and fold the bottom third over it, like a business letter. Give the dough a quarter turn and roll out again, dusting lightly with flour as necessary. Fold again into three, and wrap in plastic. Chill to rest for 20 minutes, then repeat the rolling and folding twice more. Try to remember to do the folding and turning in the same direction. Divide the dough into two or three portions as required and wrap in plastic. Use some and freeze some. Makes about 2½ pounds.

Crème anglaise

If you have never made a rich custard sauce before, you might want to have a large bowl of ice water at the ready, so you can plunge the base of the pan into it to cool the custard quickly. Another useful hint is that you can use a candy thermometer or instant-read thermometer to check if the custard is cooked enough – the temperature should be 160–170°.

Slit a vanilla bean in half and scoop out the seeds on the tip of the knife. Put 1 cup each milk and heavy cream in a heavy-based saucepan and mix in the vanilla seeds. Add the bean too. Heat until the liquid starts to rise up in the pan, then remove from the heat and allow to infuse for 10 minutes.

Meanwhile, put 6 egg yolks and ½ cup sugar in a large bowl set on a damp cloth (to hold it steady) and beat with a balloon whisk until pale golden and creamy. Remove the vanilla bean from the infused milk, then bring back to a boil. Tip in small slurps onto the sugar and yolks, whisking hard. When the mixture is well blended, return it to the pan on the lowest heat possible. Stir with a wooden spoon for about 2 minutes until the mixture starts to thicken and just coats the back of the spoon. Do not overheat or it will curdle. Strain, cover, and cool, stirring occasionally to stop a skin from forming. Makes 2½ cups.

Thyme ice cream

Heat 1 cup creamy milk and 1 cup heavy cream in a large saucepan until the liquid starts to creep up the sides of the pan. Stir in the leaves and flowers from 3 sprigs fresh thyme and leave to get cold.

Put 6 egg yolks and ½ cup sugar in a large bowl, placed on a damp cloth to hold it steady. Using a portable electric mixer, whisk the mixture until it becomes thick and creamy. Reheat the milk and cream mixture and, when the liquid rises up again, pour into the yolk mixture while whisking with the mixer running on slow. Whisk until well blended. Strain the liquid back into the pan through a sieve (discard the thyme). On the lowest heat possible, stir with a wooden spoon until the mixture thickens and coats the back of the spoon. Don't let it overheat or it will surely curdle and become grainy. Cool the custard, stirring occasionally to stop a skin from forming. (Ideally, cool quickly by standing the pan in ice water.) Churn in an electric ice cream machine until the mixture becomes a thick, swirly slush. Scoop into a plastic freezer container and freeze for a few hours, then scoop into shapes to serve. We use two teaspoons to make quenelles, but you may find a ball-shape scoop easier. Serves 4.

Fromage blanc sorbet

Tangy and pure white, this is a very refreshing palate cleanser or light accompaniment to rich sweet desserts. It is best made in an electric ice cream machine that will churn it to a creamy texture. The peppercorns add an intriguing spicy hint.

Bring 1½ cups Stock Syrup (page 214) to a boil with 4 black peppercorns, then cool and chill. Remove the peppercorns and mix in the juice of 1 lemon. Beat into 1¾ cups fromage blanc using a balloon whisk, then churn in an electric ice cream machine until creamy. Scoop into a freezer container and freeze until firm. Serve in scoops or quenelles, or, for shavings, scrape with a metal spoon. Serves 6.

Lemon sorbet

Bring 2½ cups water to a boil. Stir in 1¼ cups sugar until it dissolves, then return to a good simmer and cook for 5 minutes. Remove from the heat and stir in the the grated zest of 1 lemon and the juice of 3 lemons. Cool, then strain and chill. Churn in an ice cream machine to a soft, icy texture, then scoop into a freezer container and freeze until firm.

About 10 minutes before serving, remove from the freezer and soften at room temperature. Serves 6.

Coconut tuiles

One of our popular cookies, we serve these with all manner of desserts. We make them small and dainty, but you may prefer a more generous size.

Grind ½ cup dried shredded coconut as finely as possible in a food processor. Add ⅓ cup confectioners' sugar and 2 tablespoons all-purpose flour and whiz again to mix. Pour in 1 beaten egg white and 1 tablespoon melted butter, and process to a thick runny paste. Preheat the oven to 350°. Drop 4–6 teaspoonfuls of the coconut batter onto a baking sheet lined with parchment paper. Using a small metal spatula dipped in cold water, spread out the batter evenly and thinly to small rounds. Bake for about 7 minutes until firm, but not colored. Remove from the oven, wait a minute or so, then lift onto a wire rack to cool and crisp. Repeat with the rest of the batter. If the cookies harden before you can lift them off the baking sheet, simply return to the oven to soften for a few seconds. If you want the traditional, curved roof-tile shapes (*tuiles*), drape the warm cookies over a rolling pin and cool. Makes 12 (or 24 very dainty cookies).

Confit of orange and lemon

Heat 1 cup Stock Syrup (page 214) to boiling. Meanwhile, slice 1 large seedless orange and 1 lemon evenly into ⅛-inch disks, with the peel. Drop the fruit slices into the boiling syrup, then remove from the heat and set aside to cool.

Remove the *confit* slices as required; they can be kept in the fridge for up to a month in a covered container. When all the *confit* slices are gone, you can re-boil the syrup (it will be orange- and lemon-scented) and use again.

Praline

Preheat the oven to 350°. Warm 1⅓ cups sliced almonds in the oven for 10 minutes. Meanwhile, melt ¾ cup sugar in a saucepan with a splash of water until clear, stirring once or twice. Add a squeeze of lemon juice, then raise the heat and cook to a light caramel color. Stir in the almonds, then pour onto a flat baking sheet lined with parchment paper. Leave until cool and set. Crush with a rolling pin into chunks, then grind to very fine crumbs in a food processor. Store in a screwtop jar and use as required – praline is a delicious topping for an ice cream sundae. Makes about 10 ounces.

Preparing globe artichokes

We only use the "heart" or meaty bottom of the globe artichoke, which is enclosed in tough leaves and protected by a spiky "choke" in the center.

Once you have cut off the artichoke stalk (1), peel off the tough outer leaves with your fingers (2). Then, using a small, sharp knife, peel around the base of the artichoke to remove all the remaining leaves (3). Trim off the cream-and purple-colored inner fleshy leaves, cutting straight across just above the meaty bottom (4). Turn the artichoke bottom on its side and, with a larger cook's knife, make a straight cut downward to trim off the fine fibers of the choke (5). Finally, using the tip of a firm teaspoon, scoop out the base of the fibrous choke (6) to leave just the bottom itself. This can be cut into wedges or into thick slices (7), which can then be cut into lozenges.

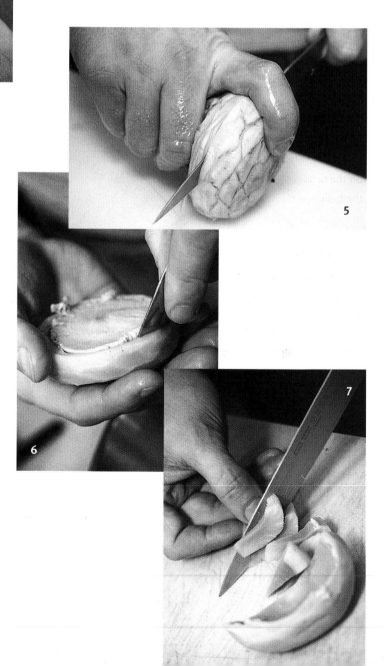

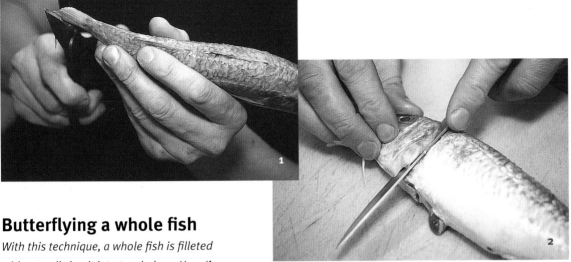

Butterflying a whole fish

With this technique, a whole fish is filleted without splitting it into two halves. Here I've butterflied a red mullet (which is used in the recipe for Baby Red Mullets with Choucroute and Rhubarb on page 184), but any small fish can be prepared in the same way. A very sharp filleting knife with a thin, flexible blade is vital, so you can make clean cuts without nicking the skin of the fish.

First, scale the fish, if the fish merchant hasn't done this for you. A red mullet has soft scales, which can be pulled off with fingers (we do this holding the fish inside a plastic bag so the scales don't fly everywhere.) Then trim the tail and main body fins with kitchen scissors (1). Cut off the head just above the gills and discard (2). Slit down the belly and pull out the innards, then rinse the fish well in cold running water, running your index finger along the blood line to make sure it is all washed away. Starting on one side of the fish and using the tip of the filleting knife, gently cut the bones away from the flesh – make shaving movements against the bones while pulling the eased flesh away with your other hand (3). Work your way back into the main body of the fish, stopping when you get to the top of the fish and the backbone. You must not cut the skin. Repeat this on the other side, working the "skeleton" free. When finished, the skeleton will still be attached to the tail. Snip the skeleton away with scissors (4), but leave the tail attached to the filleted fish. Finally, trim the edges of the butterflied fish to remove fine pin bones (5), and run the tips of your fingers across the flesh to check there are no more bones left.

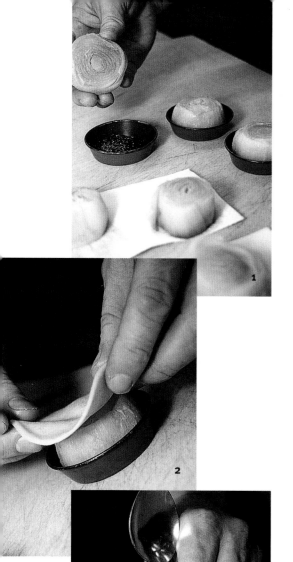

Making endive tarts

These pretty little tarts, used in the recipe for Duck Breasts with Endive Tarts on page 190, are a savory version of tarte Tatin. There are three elements – a balsamic-flavored caramel, the base of an endive head, and a small disk of puff pastry.

Make the caramel and pour it into the molds. Trim each endive head so you are left with a dumpy base about 1¼ inches tall. (The tips can be used in salads). Place an endive base, widest side down, in each mold so it is nicely submerged in the caramel (1). Set a pastry disk on top (2) and tuck it neatly around the endive using the end of a small spoon (3). After baking, unmold the tarts onto a plate. To enhance the attractive rose effect, separate the endive leaves slightly with the spoon handle (4).

Shaving corn kernels off the cob

Very fresh corn kernels are deliciously tender and juicy. When corn is in season, I like to shave the kernels off the cob to use in a dish such as Corn and Green Onion Risotto (page 68). The kernels also make mighty fine nibbling if you are a bit hungry – they're lower in fat than peanuts!

After stripping off the green leaves and silky golden strands, cut off the pointed end of the cob. Stand the ear on end on a wooden board, cut end down and slightly at an angle. Hold the ear firmly by the stalk. Using a sharp cook's knife, cut straight down the ear to remove the kernels in a line. They will probably fly everywhere, so work slowly and carefully. After each cut, turn the ear slightly. Repeat until all the sweet juicy kernels are freed. (The spent cobs can be used in a vegetable *nage*.)

Making fennel fans

Lots of trimming, peeling, and slashing are needed for this, but the technique is actually quite simple, and the end result is very attractive. I serve these in a dish of Red Mullet with Orange-Glazed Fennel and Pesto Dressing (page 136).

First, trim off the stalks and feathery fronds (1) – you can use these in other dishes or the fronds as garnish. The outer segments of fennel benefit from a light peeling to make them more tender, so shave off the tough outer ribs with a small, sharp paring knife (2). Place the shaved and trimmed fennel bulb upright on a board and cut firmly in half (3). Using the small knife, cut out the base core from each half in a neat "V" shape (4), but keep the root end intact so the layers of the fennel half still hold together. After braising in buttery stock until tender, transfer the fennel halves to a board, placing them cut-side down. With the tip of a cook's knife, slash each half evenly (5), leaving the root end uncut to hold the "fan" together. Lift the fennel halves onto warmed plates with a metal spatula and gently press the slashed flesh to separate and open up the fan (6).

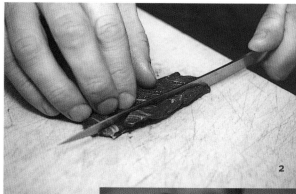

Making gnocchi

Potato gnocchi are fun and easy to make, and are delicious with a warm salad of peas and fèves (page 24) or rabbit slow-cooked in goose fat (page 145). The potatoes should be quite dry, so either bake them or dry them out in the oven after boiling.

Mix the mashed potato with flour, egg, and the other ingredients to a firm but still soft dough, then divide into balls the size of a small apple. On a lightly floured board, roll out each ball to a cigar shape about 10 inches long (1). Flatten the cigar slightly to an oval shape. Using either the back of a table knife or a blunt cook's knife, cut across in 1¼-inch lengths, cutting slightly on the diagonal (2). This will give the gnocchi their characteristic pinched edges. Cook the gnocchi as soon as they have been cut, so they don't have time to dry out.

Making steak tartare

For a perfectly made steak tartare you must have the finest quality beef. Mine is Scottish, of course, the very best on the market. The meat must be chopped just once so it retains a clean texture and taste – aggressive chopping and, even worse, grinding, which mangles up the flesh, will destroy the eating quality of the beef and make it taste "cooked." My recipe for steak tartare is on page 197.

First, trim any vestige of fat from the beef, then cut into thin slices (1). Cut each slice into thin strips (2). Gather a few strips together and cut them across into tiny, tiny cubes (3). Transfer the finely minced beef to a metal bowl set in a larger bowl containing ice water (4) so that it will be chilled quickly. Finish by mixing in the flavoring ingredients and then shaping into patties.

1

2

3

4

Making towers

This is a very simple presentation technique that gives an attractive professional finish. It can be used for all sorts of dishes, from creamy risottos and creamed root purées to layers of vegetables topped with fish fillets or neat pieces of meat. Here I'm layering the crab cocktail for the Pepper and Tomato Soup on page 64. You need a deep, straight-sided metal ring such as a plain biscuit cutter.

Set the cutter in the middle of the plate or soup bowl and spoon in the first layer – here crushed avocado (1). Spread this smooth with the back of the spoon (2). Then add the next layer, which is crab salad (3), and press it down gently (4). Finish with a float of cocktail sauce. Hold your breath and ease the cutter up and away (5). Wipe it clean and start with the next plate.

5

Index

Acknowledgments

A book of this quality doesn't just happen overnight, although the Quadrille staff have displayed mind-blowing efficiency and skill in ensuring tight deadlines have been met. I am in complete awe of the quality of their work. So big thanks to everyone involved: Roz Denny for her quiet determination and cunning in keeping me working (roughly) to the schedule and ingenious ways of extracting information from me; Mark Sargeant, one of my indispensable staff, for working alongside me at the photo shoots, sacrificing his weekend biker outings (no greater love hath a sous chef for his master); Georgia Glynn Smith, forever stunning and calm, with the most focused right eye in the business, for producing true art that has taken my breath away; Helen Lewis for her clear and clever design and making sure I was on time for the Saturday shoots; Norma MacMillan (project editor) for her thoroughness, professionalism, and gentle persuasive manner in making sure it all happened when it was supposed to; and Anne Furniss at Quadrille for her enthusiasm and faith in me.

But perhaps the biggest thanks should go to two of the most important women in my life – my P.A., Carla Pastorino, who gently but firmly controls and influences every aspect of my working life; and my sweet, sexy wife, Tana. Her tolerance has enabled me to work on Saturdays when I did promise to be at home to help her with young Megan and the "Tweenies." In return I make this promise to start cooking Sunday lunches for her and the children, when they are all old enough to sit up at the table.